THE LAST
BYZANTINE RENAISSANCE

THE WILES LECTURES
GIVEN AT THE QUEEN'S UNIVERSITY
BELFAST 1968

THE
LAST BYZANTINE
RENAISSANCE

STEVEN RUNCIMAN

CAMBRIDGE
AT THE UNIVERSITY PRESS
1970

Published by the Syndics of the Cambridge University Press
Bentley House, 200 Euston Road, London N.W.1
American Branch: 32 East 57th Street, New York, N.Y.10022

© Cambridge University Press 1970

Standard Book Number: 521 07787 7

Printed in Great Britain
at the University Printing House, Cambridge
(Brooke Crutchley, University Printer)

CONTENTS

PREFACE

This book is made up of four lectures delivered at the Queen's University, Belfast, under the aegis of the Wiles Trust. They are printed much as they were delivered, with some slight re-arrangement and the verbal alterations needed when the spoken word is transformed into the written word. One of the features of the Wiles Lectureship is that scholars interested in the subject of the lectures are invited not only to attend them but promptly to criticize what the lecturer has said. I have profited from that salutary experience and have made a few further emendations in my text.

The nature of my subject precludes startling original research. It has, rather, been my aim to try to correlate and to put into perspective the intellectual achievements of the last two centuries of the Byzantine Empire, when the State was collapsing but learning never shone more brightly. I have made one serious omission. It would have taken too much time and space to have included a worthy discussion of the art that was the most splendid achievement of the period. The product of Byzantine scholars is less attractive to us today than the product of Byzantine artists. But scholarship should be judged by the standards of its age, not by the tastes of subsequent generations.

I have to confess that I have not read every word of the works of scholarship about which I am writing. That would be the task of a lifetime, especially as many of them are unpublished and not easily accessible nor easily legible. I am dependent for my knowledge of them to the labours of scholars who have studied them. Though I have tried at least to glance at the accessible printed works, I must admit that I have not had the time nor the enthusiasm needed to wade through the endless commentaries of ancient works of which the Byzantines were so proud, and whose style is for the most part distinguished for verbosity and elaboration. There are, indeed, writers amongst them whose works can be read with pleasure, such as Cabasilas and Demetrius Cydones; but they are in the minority.

Not wishing the text to be dwarfed by the reference-notes, I have kept the latter as short as possible. In particular, when dealing with individual scholars, I have avoided long bibliographical details but have preferred to refer to secondary works where such information can be easily found. My notes bear witness to the debt that I owe to such works. In transliterating Greek names I have kept to the traditional old Latin system, except where the name is more familiar in another form.

I should like to express my thanks to Mrs Janet P. Boyd, to whose generosity the Wiles Lectures owe their existence; to the Vice-Chancellor of the Queen's University and Mrs Vick, to Professor Michael

Roberts, and to other friends in Belfast who also gave me hospitality and help. And it is a special pleasure to me that the publication of the Wiles Lectures is assigned to the Cambridge University Press, to whose helpful friendship I have long been indebted.

STEVEN RUNCIMAN

Elshieshields, Dumfriesshire, 1969

1

IMPERIAL DECLINE AND
HELLENIC REVIVAL

IF THERE IS any meaning in the concept of decadence, there are few polities in history that better deserve to be called decadent than the East Christian Empire, the once great Roman Empire, during the last two centuries of its existence. It was a period when a crumbling administration, directed by an inept and short-sighted government and centred in a city whose population was rapidly diminishing, vainly attempted to ward off increasing impoverishment and the steady loss of territory. The irresponsible ambitions of its leaders encouraged disastrous civil wars. Militarily and economically the decline was rapid. The Emperor himself was poorer and feebler than most of the princes whose domains surrounded him, and he was soon to become the vassal of an infidel master. The political history of Byzantium under the Emperors of the Palaeologan dynasty is a tale of folly and misery, until at last the *coup de grâce* of 1453 comes almost as a relief.

Yet was it a period of decadence? In strange contrast with the political decline, the intellectual life of Byzantium never shone so brilliantly as in those two sad centuries. In the sphere of art the earlier Palaeologan period was of supreme importance; and if the artistic output faltered and failed as time went on, that was due to the lack of material resources, not of inspiration. It was an age of eager and erudite philosophers, culminating in its later years in the most original of all Byzantine thinkers, George Gemistus Plethon. The previous generation had produced the finest mystical exegetist of the Eastern Church in Gregory Palamas. There was a sequence of ingenious scientists, whose discoveries, however, could not find practical expression because of the poverty of the State. At no other epoch was Byzantine society so highly educated and so deeply interested in things of the intellect and the spirit.

The contrast is not easy to explain. Maybe we should look at it in reverse. Intellectuals are seldom good administrators. Had there been fewer of them in high places the government might have been more competent. The subjects of the cultured Emperor Andronicus might well have longed for a ruler less devotedly concerned with culture, such as the great Basil II. A civil service chosen for its high scholarship is not always the most effective. To quarrel passionately over the doctrine of the Energies of God when the enemy is overrunning the countryside and plague devastating the cities shows a sense of priorities admirable in the truly religious but unsuited for practical efficiency. Was it that the intense piety which had always inspired the Byzantine interest in philosophy and theology had now grown too great? Or was it a vicious circle? The more that the Byzantines concentrated on the intellect and the spirit the less able they were to meet the challenge of the outside world: while their failure to meet the challenge induced them, in the deepening gloom, to devote themselves more and more to the things that mattered for the world to come.

It is impossible to understand the Byzantines without remembering their piety. Every one of them firmly believed that this world was only a prelude to a better world in which he would share if he remained true to the Faith. He was not unaware of this world. In his personal actions he was full of practical and not always very ethical good sense; and his political dealings were often very astute. Byzantine diplomacy showed to the end a cynical appreciation of the human weaknesses of foreign statesmen and foreign peoples. But in his worldly dealings he was apt to look for immediate results. His longer view was dominated by his piety, which could easily lead to defeatism and even apathy when things went wrong. The disasters that befell the Empire were seen as divine punishment for the sins of its citizens. They were therefore inevitable and just. This belief did not prevent the Byzantines from continuing to sin. In particular the princes and magnates never ceased from indulging their ambitions by intrigue or even by open rebellion, and by behaviour that in any other society would have ranked as treason.

The melancholy sequence of political events certainly suggested that sin was rampant. It is fashionable amongst present-day Byzantine historians to play down the effects of the Latin capture of Constantinople in 1204.[1] The doom of the Empire was sealed earlier, at Manzikert and by the Turkish invasions, and the loss to the Empire of its economic and demographic heartlands in Anatolia. That may be true; and, if we wish, we can go further back and trace the decline to the ineffectual social and economic policy of the administration of the mid-eleventh century. But the search for earlier causes does not lessen the terrible effect that the events of 1204 had on Byzantium, politically and morally. New Rome, the Imperial City, the home of the Emperors and the centre of their government, had fallen into the hands of hated and despised Westerners. Not only was the whole physical organization of the Empire ruined, but the humiliation was bitter and unforgettable. The sacred Imperial power was driven into exile; and even in exile it was divided, with claimants in Nicaea, in Epirus and in Trebizond; and even though the Nicaean Emperors eliminated the rivalry of the Epirotes, Trebizond remained as a separate en-

[1] See the introduction to the *Cambridge Medieval History*, IV, part I (new edition, 1966), x.

tity and even survived Constantinople, with which its relationship was always a little equivocal. When the Nicaeans liberated Constantinople and re-established the Empire in its proper capital, it was not the same Empire. It no longer represented the Christian East. It was merely one State amongst others in the Levant; and most of the others were materially more powerful. The Imperial title still maintained a curious mystical prestige; Balkan monarchs were eager to have their own titles recognized by the Emperor; and this prestige was backed by the prestige of the great city and its great church and its historic Patriarchate. But even the Imperial prestige was fading. In about 1395 the Patriarch Anthony of Constantinople had to write to the Great Prince Basil I of Russia to remind him that, though the Empire was reduced to tragic straits, the Emperor was still the Holy Emperor, the head of the Orthodox commonwealth.[1] The old conception of the Christian Empire was becoming a myth.

Nevertheless, the shock of the disaster of 1204 seemed to give new force to the intellectual vitality of the Byzantines. It is interesting, if idle, to speculate on what might have happened had the Latin Empire of Romania produced other Emperors of the calibre of Henry of Flanders, men who sincerely sought to reconcile and absorb their Orthodox subjects, or even

[1] F. Miklosich and L. Müller, *Acta et Diplomata Graeca Medii Aevi* (6 vols., Vienna, 1860–90), II, 188–92.

had Henry himself lived longer, or had the Roman Church shown greater flexibility and sympathy in dealing with the Greeks. Possibly then the majority of the Greeks might have accepted the new order, and a Greco-Latin synthesis might have evolved. But, as it was, the livelier elements in the Greek intellectual world went into exile, a few into the seclusion of monasteries and the rest to one or other of the Greek succession-states, eventually gathering round the Court at Nicaea, which seems to have the best claim to legitimacy and to offer the best hopes for the future.

Backed as it was by many of the best Greek brains of the time, the Nicaean Empire suggested that the Byzantines were recovering both their practical talent for government and their moral confidence. The Empire was well administered, with realistic common-sense and homely thrift. Where else could one find an Emperor making enough money out of his poultry-keeping to buy his Empress a new crown? The Nicaean diplomats showed the traditional Byzantine skill in taking advantage of their enemies' rivalries and quarrels; and they were helped by the temporary weakness of the Turks, whose eyes were necessarily turned eastward, towards the menacing Mongols. The Court was highly cultured, and the Emperors were all of them men who commanded respect. Meanwhile the Latin Empire was sinking further and further into ineptitude. No one can have been greatly surprised when in 1261 troops from Nicaea recovered Constantinople.[1]

It was with happy hopes for the future that the Empire was reinstated in its sacred and historic capital. But the reconquest created new problems. It roused schemes of revenge among the Western powers. It caused difficulties with the Italian sea-port cities whose merchants had taken control of the international trade of the city and were not to be dislodged. The city itself had to be administered and fed and protected from the ambitions of the Balkan princes. The government was so anxiously concerned with potential dangers from the Balkans and from the West that it began to neglect the Eastern frontier. There the Turks had long been quiescent, but now a vigorous new emirate was emerging, led by Osman and his successors. The Empire was to pay heavily for this neglect.

The Emperor Michael Palaeologus, the recoverer of Constantinople, saw the Empire safely through the immediate crises. The Empire was still rich. The thrift of the Nicaeans had left the treasury full. The Italian capture of the carrying trade did not destroy but, rather, enhanced the importance of the markets in Constantinople: while Thessalonica, the second city of the Empire, prospered as the chief port of the Balkans.

---

[1] For the Nicaean Empire, see *Cambridge Medieval History*, IV, part 1, ch. VII (by D. M. Nicol), 295 ff.; also A. Gardner, *The Lascarids of Nicaea* (London, 1912), *passim*.

Michael's diplomacy was aided by his discreet use of money. The plot culminating in the massacre of the Sicilian Vespers, in which he was deeply involved, lessened the danger from the West; and his intrigues kept the Serbian and Bulgarian rulers from threatening his dominions and enabled him to recover lands in the Greek peninsula from the Franks. But he left the Empire divided internally. He was an usurper, and he had promised to maintain the rights and welfare of the young legitimate Emperor, John IV. When he brutally broke his promise, the Patriarch Arsenius excommunicated him, and he in his turn dethroned the Patriarch. This caused a schism in the Church. While most of the hierarchs were prepared to forgive him once he had made an act of contrition, many of the lesser clergy and the monks, who were always resentful of Imperial control of the Church, continued to regard him as excommunicated and Arsenius as Patriarch. The Arsenites, as they were called from their somewhat unwilling leader, formed for a generation a party that refused to co-operate with the State; but after Michael's death in 1282 they faded out.

But meanwhile Michael's policy had led to a more lasting division. In his desire to ward off attacks from the West he decided that it would be politically desirable for the Church of Constantinople to re-unite itself with the Church of Rome, even though Rome demanded the submission of Constantinople as the price of union. His policy stirred up a controversy that was to last, with varying intensity, until the fall of the Empire in 1453. Henceforward, while every thinking Byzantine had to make up his mind whether or not his Church ought to submit to Rome, the Byzantine man in the street, to whom the idea was repugnant, turned against any Emperor or minister who sought to further the union.[1]

After Michael's death the Empire, politically and economically, began to run steadily downhill. His son and successor, Andronicus II, was a highly educated man of great personal charm, but ineffectual as a ruler. He restored peace amongst his subjects by reconciling the Arsenites and by repudiating the union with Rome that his father had accepted at the Council of Lyons. But the Ottoman Turks now presented a threat that could not be ignored; and his attempt to curb them by hiring the services of the disreputable Catalan Company resulted in the Company devastating his own territory and doing nothing to stem the Turkish advance. He could not prevent the ominous rise of the Serbian kingdom. He could not control his own relations or his ministers. Eventually, after a reign distinguished for its cultural and artistic activities but otherwise disastrous, he began to lose his earlier

---

[1] See *Cambridge Medieval History*, IV, part I, ch. VIII (by G. Ostrogorsky), 332–40; L. Petit, article 'Arsène Autorianus et Arsénites', in *Dictionnaire de Théologie catholique* (ed. A. Vacant, E. Mangeot and others), I, part II, cols I. 1911–14.

popularity. His eldest son predeceased him; but his grandson, Andronicus III, led the opposition against him, and, after seven years of fitful civil war, deposed him in 1328.

Andronicus III, ably helped by his chief minister, John Cantacuzenus, was a more vigorous ruler under whom the Empire won some successes in Thessaly and Greece. But the civil war had been debilitating. The Turks continued to advance in Asia and the Serbs in Europe. When he died in 1341 only a few isolated towns were left to the Empire in Asia, and the Serbians were at the gates of Thessalonica. The fifty-year reign of Andronicus's son, John V (1341–91), was a period of unceasing disaster. John, who was ten years old at the time of his accession, was removed from power in the course of it by his father-in-law, his son and his grandson, though he was never actually deposed and died as Emperor.

The reign began with a civil war of six years' duration, when John Cantacuzenus, deprived of his expectancy of the regency by the intrigues of the Empress-Mother, Anna of Savoy, and of the Patriarch, John Calecas, resorted to arms and was eventually recognized as John V's senior colleague in the Empire, the young Emperor marrying his daughter. But John VI Cantacuzenus was unseated in a plot in 1354 and spent the rest of his long life as a monk, but treated also as an elder statesman. John V then governed feebly for nineteen years, to be unseated by his eldest son, Andronicus IV, for a few months in 1373 and again from 1376 to 1379. Andronicus continued to plot until his death in 1385; and in 1390 John VII, the son of Andronicus, drove his aged grandfather into retirement for nearly a year.[1]

The plots and civil wars were disastrous for the Empire. They used up its wealth; they dislocated trade; and neither side had any scruple about inviting foreign forces to intervene. As a result, the Turks were able to establish themselves in Europe in the 1340s and by 1360 controlled the whole province of Thrace. The power of Serbia grew and might have overwhelmed the Empire had not disorders followed the death of the great Serbian monarch, Stephen Dushan, in 1355. In the end it was the Turks who destroyed the Serbian menace. They annexed the greater part of Bulgaria during the years that followed their great victory over the Serbian and Bulgarian armies on the River Maritsa in 1371, and most of Serbia after their still greater victory at Kossovo in 1389. By the time of John V's death the Turkish dominions had reached the River Danube, and the Christian Empire consisted of little more than Constantinople itself, a few sea-ports strung along the Balkan coastline, a few small islands in the

[1] For a summary of the civil wars, see *Cambridge Medieval History*, IV, part I, ch. VIII, 340–73. I think that the author, Ostrogorsky, somewhat overstresses the social issues.

Aegean Sea, and the Peloponnese, ruled by cadets of the Imperial family, where alone Byzantine arms and diplomacy had met with some success. Thessalonica had been temporarily held by the Turks in 1387 and was annexed by them in 1394. Since about 1375 the Emperor had acknowledged the suzerainty of the Turkish Sultan.[1]

Visitations of the plague had helped to ruin the economy and the well-being of the Empire. The Black Death struck Constantinople in 1347. Horrified contemporaries declared that nine-tenths of its population perished. Allowing for medieval exaggerations it is probable that the population of the city did decline by nearly a half, and that of the whole Empire by about a third. Though the neighbouring Turks and Balkan peoples suffered too, their more rural economy made their losses not quite so severe.[2]

Social problems added to the chaos. The civil war between John Cantacuzenus and the government of the Empress Anna has been explained as a struggle between the landed magnates and the urban proletariat. This view is, I think, an oversimplification. If we examine the reactions of the Byzantines of whom we know some-

[1] The best short summary of early Ottoman history is in P. Wittek, *The Rise of the Ottoman Empire* (London, 1938). See also N. Jorga, *Geschichte des Osmanischen Reiches* (5 vols., Gotha, 1908–13), vol. I; M. F. Köprülü, *Les Origines de l'Empire Ottoman* (Paris, 1935); I. H. Üzüncarşîlî, *Osmanlî Tarihi* (3 vols., Ankara, 1947–51), vol. I.
[2] See S. Runciman, *The Fall of Constantinople* (Cambridge, 1965), p. 5 and n. 1 (p. 205) giving references.

thing, we find that each reacted individually to individual questions, without following any consistent party-line. There was certainly hostility between the poorer citizens of the cities and the landed aristocracy that ran the government; but it was affected more by religion than by politics, while personalities counted for more than policies. There were indeed massacres of the magnates in the course of the civil wars in several cities; and the Zealot rising in Thessalonica, which gave those municipal rebels control of their city from 1342 to 1349 and disrupted its hitherto prosperous life, was accompanied by class bloodshed. But even there it is impossible to distinguish the social from the religious issues and unwise to ignore the clash of personalities.[1]

The fourteenth century was thus for Byzantium a century of decline from which recovery was impossible. The admirable efforts of the Emperor Manuel II, who succeeded his father John V in 1391, were fruitless, even though the Turks were checked for a time by the invasion of Anatolia by Timur the Tartar and his victory over the Sultan at Ankara. Byzantium was given a respite. A few cities, including Thessalonica, were restored to Imperial rule: though Thessalonica was sold by its despairing governor to the Venetians in 1423, and the Turks re-annexed it in 1430. Manuel himself,

[1] See *Cambridge Medieval History*, IV, part 1, ch. VIII, 357–62; P. Charanis, 'Internal Strife in Byzantium in the fourteenth century', in *Byzantion*, XV (Boston, 1940–1), 208–30; O. Tafrali, *Thessalonique au quatorzième siècle* (Paris, 1913), pp. 225–72.

till the close of his reign, when his son, John VIII, had taken over the government, kept on fairly good terms with the Turks. But Constantinople and the Empire itself were clearly doomed. The reign of John VIII (1425–48), was dominated by the question of union with Rome, the policy which the Emperor believed might bring aid that could perhaps save the Empire, but which was rejected even so by most of his subjects. The end came under John's brother and successor, Constantine XI, when a vigorous and brilliant young Sultan, Mehmet II, to be surnamed the Conqueror, organized and administered the final blow.[1]

This is the background against which we must see the scholars of Palaeologan Constantinople. It is a period that begins with a short-lived feeling of hope, after the recovery of the capital from the Latins, but which soon sinks into disorder and disillusion and at last despair. How was it that the intellectual life could burgeon so splendidly?

The disaster of 1204 provided the first stimulus. The Byzantines had always been conscious of their Greek past. They might call themselves Romans and remember proudly that theirs was the legitimate Roman Empire. Still more, they were Christians, to whom pagan learning was of secondary importance in comparison with the Christian revelation. But their

[1] *Cambridge Medieval History*, IV, part 2, ch. VIII, 378–87; Runciman, *Fall of Constantinople*, pp. 12–21, 48–72.

language was Greek, their literature written in Greek; and the works of the ancient Greek world were still studied and admired. Homer was to them 'the Poet', quotations from whose poems were expected to be immediately recognized and appreciated.[1] Plato and Aristotle were to them teachers with whose philosophy anyone with a claim to education must have some acquaintance. Their sciences all rested on old Classical foundations.[2] But the word 'Hellene' was to be avoided, as it carried the meaning of 'Pagan'. The Byzantine child had to 'hellenize' his tongue (as Anna Comnena words it); that is to say, he had to learn to write Greek in a Classical style with a Classical vocabulary. The study of rhetoric, as this discipline was called, was a necessary part of a full education. But the language taught in it was far removed from the spoken tongue. It aimed at Attic purity, but it became far too often an artificial *katharevousa*, flowery and verbose. In

[1] In the *Alexiad* Anna Comnena makes sixty-six references to the works of Homer and clearly expects her readers to catch the allusions without further explanation. She rarely bothers to add: 'as the Poet says...'. See G. Buckler, *Anna Comnena* (Oxford, 1929), pp. 197–200. Psellus (*History*, ed. C. Sathas, London, 1899, pp. 116–17) tells the story of a compliment paid to the Lady Scleraena by a courtier who had only to mention the first two words of the passage describing Helen passing along the walls of Troy for his allusion to be taken.

[2] If we take Anna Comnena again as a typical well-educated Byzantine, we find that she claims to have studied Aristotle and Plato, but she does not actually display very much knowledge of the latter, and much of her information about Greek learning seems to come from Plutarch (see Buckler, *Anna Comnena*, pp. 202–8). For the sciences, see below, pp. 88–93.

defence of rhetoric we should remember that, in the days before printing, a book if it was to circulate at all widely would have to be read aloud, the number of manuscripts being limited; and a concise style, however agreeable to an individual reader, is often difficult for a listener to follow. A wordier style suits him better. But, unfortunately, too many Byzantine writers became intoxicated by words and wrote with such elaboration that neither reader nor listener could easily comprehend the meaning.[1]

This education enabled a Byzantine to read the Classics; and the Classics were read. It is true that the Byzantines had a love for compilations and encyclopedias, short cuts to learning. But this love should not be exaggerated. The originals were not neglected. Indeed, when making quotations, they were all too often apt to rely upon faulty memories and not to consult their dictionary of quotations.[2]

The cult of the Classics was thus nothing new. It had been encouraged by the Iconoclastic Emperors. It had been actively patronized by Constantine Prophyrogenitus and by the cultured Emperors of the eleventh century. During the twelfth century the scholarship

[1] Anna Comnena, *Alexiad*, ed. B. Leib (Paris, 1937), I, preface, 4. See Buckler, *Anna Comnena*, pp. 499–500.
[2] Books such as Photius's *Myriobiblion* and Suidas's *Lexicon* were undoubtedly popular in Byzantium; and the scholars all enjoyed making compendiums of learning (see below, lecture 3, *passim*.) But the originals had to be carefully studied before compendiums could be made.

became a little more profound. The commentaries on Classical authors made by John Tzetzes, who was born early in the century, cover an enormous range and show enormous erudition, though to modern eyes they may seem naive and superficial, and are unsuitably written in indifferent verse.[1] In the next generation Eustathius, Metropolitan of Thessalonica, a pious and active hierarch, found time to write a commentary on Homer which is first class and still of value; and he also studied Hesiod.[2] At the end of the century Michael Acominatus, Metropolitan of Athens, was a Classical humanist whose sensitive appreciation of past literature is reflected in the easy elegance of his letters. Though he was a sincere Christian, to whom 'Hellene' still meant 'pagan', he felt himself to be of the same mould as the Hellenes.[3]

This consciousness of the Hellenic inheritance was enhanced by the Latin Conquest and the exile in Nicaea. Byzantium still claimed to be the Roman

[1] For Tzetzes, see K. Krumbacher, *Geschichte der Byzantinischen Litteratur* (2nd ed., Munich, 1897), pp. 526–36; A. A. Vasiliev, *History of the Byzantine Empire* (Madison, 1952), pp. 498–500.

[2] Krumbacher, *Byzantinischen Litteratur*, pp. 536–41; P. Koukoules, 'Λαογραφικαὶ εἰδήσεις παρὰ τῷ Θεσσαλονίκης Εὐσταθίῳ', 'Επετηρὶς 'Εταιρείας Βυζαντινῶν Σπουδῶν, I (Athens, 1924), 5–40. Eustathius's works are published in L. F. Tafel, *Eustathii Metropolitae Thessalonicensis Opuscula* (Frankfurt, 1832).

[3] Krumbacher, *Byzantinischen Litteratur*, pp. 468–70; H.-G. Beck, *Kirche und theologische Literatur im Byzantinischen Reich* (Munich, 1959), pp. 637–8; G. Stadmüller, *Michael Choniates, Metropolit von Athen* (Rome, 1934), *passim*.

Empire; but the claim must have begun to sound a little hollow to men who saw Westerners controlling New Rome and Old Rome itself at the centre of an ebullient civilization. The Westerners had defeated and humiliated Byzantium; but there was one thing that they could not take away and that they could not as yet share; and that was the Greek tradition. On their side the Westerners began to realize something of the wealth of Greek learning. They discovered that in the Greek lands which they had invaded, Aristotle, the philosopher whom they were beginning to admire so greatly, could be read and studied in his original words, and Plato too, and other philosophers whose names they knew. They despised the Greeks around them, but they could not despise Greek learning. It was natural that the Greeks should make use of this asset. They were proud to be Greeks. The word 'Hellene' began to lose its pejorative connotation.

It is possible that demographic reasons aided the change in sentiment. The loss to Byzantium of central Anatolia and the Balkan hinterland reduced the Empire to territories that had been Greek since the dawn of history, lands in the Greek peninsula itself and along the coasts of the Aegean and the Euxine and in the islands, where the earliest Greek colonies had been settled. Greek blood had been mixed even in Classical times and had become far more mixed in the cosmopolitan centuries that followed the conquests of Alexander the Great and the oecumenical centuries of Rome and the Later Roman Empire. But now the Byzantines, concentrated in historic Greek territories, could know themselves to be geographically Greek and could imagine themselves to be racially Greek.

It was not, however, until the mid-fourteenth century that Byzantine writers dared to make use of the word 'Hellene' to describe themselves.[1] In the great speech that the Emperor Michael VIII made at Nymphaeum a few days before his triumphant entry into Constantinople, a speech which contains the germ of the later *Megali Idea*, the doctrine that the Greeks are a race specially endowed down the ages by the grace of God to take the lead, politically and intellectually in Europe and in Asia, he was thinking of old Greek traditions but he referred to his people as the Romans— *Rhomaioi*—while the citizens of Rome itself were merely called Italians, *Italoi*.[2] Even in the later fourteenth century intellectuals such as the ex-Emperor

---

[1] Professor R. Browning has had the kindness to inform me that he has found one instance in the twelfth century of the use of 'Hellene' to mean 'contemporary Greek'. For the Byzantine use of 'Hellene', see S. Runciman, 'Byzantine and Hellene in the fourteenth century', Τόμος Κωνσταντίνου ᾽Αρμενοπούλου (Thessalonica, 1952), pp. 27–31; H. Ditten, 'Βάρβαροι, ῝Ελληνες und ῾Ρωμαῖοι bei den letzten byzantinischen Geschichtsschreibern', *Actes du XIIe. Congrès International d'Etudes Byzantines* (Belgrade, 1964), II, 273–99. Metochites uses 'Hellene' to denote a man educated in Hellenic learning. See below, p. 87, n. 1.

[2] G. Pachymer, *De Michaele et Andronico Palaeologis*, ed. I. Bekker (Bonn, 1835), pp. 153–5, 159.

19

John Cantacuzenus, who was perhaps a little conservative in his views, and Nicephorus Gregoras, who regarded himself as completely up-to-date, still use 'Hellenic' to describe the old pagan learning as opposed to the 'inner' learning of Christian theology.

The new use of 'Hellene' seems to have been inaugurated in Thessalonica. Thessalonica had always been a Greek city, without the Imperial oecumenical traditions of Constantinople. Its hierarchs had in the distant past, it is true, been the exarchs of the Roman pontiffs in the East. But they liked to forget that they owed their prefix of 'Holiness' to that position. The schools of Thessalonica had long been centres for Classical learning; and the work and influence of the great Metropolitan Eustathius had enhanced their reputation. By the end of the thirteenth century a large proportion of the leading Byzantine scholars were Thessalonians by birth or by upbringing. It is in the writings of one of the most distinguished members of this Thessalonian milieu that we first find the new use of the word 'Hellene'. In an eloquent encomium of Saint Demetrius, patron saint of the city, which Nicholas Cabasilas wrote as a young man, in about 1348, he describes Thessalonica as the second Athens, the home of the Hellenes of his day; and, in a covering letter that he sent with a copy of the encomium from Constantinople where he was living to his father in Thessalonica, he expresses his misgivings in letting him see the work for fear that its inelegant language might shock 'you Hellenes'.[1]

Cabasilas there uses the word in a cultural sense, but without any suggestion that Hellenes were to be equated with pagans. Soon, more significantly, we find the word used in a racial sense. Nicephorus Gregoras kept up a correspondence with a Cypriot scholar, Athanasius Lepenthrenus, from whom he wanted to find out what remained of ancient Greek splendours in Cyprus and in other places which Lepenthrenus, who was an eager traveller, had visited. Gregoras is careful in his terminology; but Lepenthrenus, in a letter written in about 1355, speaks openly of 'all the Hellenes here in Cyprus', and goes on later, when speaking of other lands, to mention 'everywhere where Hellenes live'.[2]

Very soon afterwards we find Demetrius Cydones, who, like Cabasilas, was born and brought up in Thessalonica, though of Cretan origin, using 'Hellas' to mean the Byzantine Empire. In a later letter Cabasilas follows his example.[3] By the fifteenth century the usage was fairly general. In about 1440 John Argyropoulos wrote of the struggle for the freedom of 'Hellas'

---

[1] MS. Gr. Paris 1213, fos. 47–8, 294, quoted in Tafrali, *Thessalonique au quatorzième siècle*, pp. 156, n. 3, 169, n. 1.

[2] *Correspondance de Nicéphore Grégoras*, ed. R. Guilland (Paris, 1927), p. 285.

[3] Demetrius Cydones, *Correspondance*, ed. G. Cammelli (Paris, 1930), pp. 18, 30; MS. Gr. *cit.*, fol. 301, in Tafrali, *Thessalonique au quatorzième siècle*, p. 157, n. 2 (letter of Cabasilas to the Empress Anna).

in a letter addressed to John VIII as 'Emperor of Hellas'.[1] We have come a long way from the days when the ambassador Liudprand of Cremona was thought unfit to be received at the Court because his credentials were addressed to the 'Emperor of the Greeks'. But 'Graeci' was never an acceptable term. George Scholarius, the future Patriarch Gennadius, who was to be the link between the old Byzantine world and the world of the Turcocratia, often uses 'Hellene' to mean anyone of Greek blood. But he had doubts about its propriety; he still retained the older view. When he was asked his specific opinion about his race, he wrote in reply: 'Though I am a Hellene by birth, yet I would never say that I was a Hellene. For I do not believe as the Hellenes believed. I should like to take my name from my faith and, if anyone asked me what I am, to reply "a Christian". Though my father dwelt in Thessaly,' he adds, 'I do not call myself a Thessalian, but a Byzantine. For I am of Byzantium.'[2] It is to be remarked that though he repudiates the name of Hellene he calls the Imperial City not New Rome or Constantinople, but by its old Hellenic name.

This revolutionary revival of the word 'Hellene' gives a clue to the nature of the last Byzantine Renaissance. It was a Greek, a Hellenic, renaissance. With their political power crumbling around them the

[1] S. P. Lambros, ᾽Αργυροπουλεία (Athens, 1910), pp. 4–7.
[2] G. Scholarius Gennadius, 'Contre les Juifs', in *Oeuvres Complètes* (Paris, 1928–36), III, 252.

Byzantines clung to their great cultural asset. In a world where ancient Greek learning was increasingly admired they could claim that they were Greeks, the heirs in unbroken succession to the poets and philosophers, the historians and scientists of ancient Hellas; and the claim carried them proudly on. Ethnologists may question the racial basis of the claim, theologians point out the difference in culture that Christianity had brought; and historians may reflect that an Athenian gentleman of the fifth century B.C. would have felt far from home in Constantinople of the fifteenth century A.D. Yet the claim was not illegitimate. The Greek world of the last two centuries of Byzantium had shrunk now to become little more than a group of city-states, Constantinople, Thessalonica, Trebizond and Mistra. It had become, far more truly than Byzantium in its grand Imperial days, the descendant of the city-states of the ancient Hellenic world, and it showed the same intellectual vivacity and bustle.

3-2

2

CONTROVERSY AND FACTION

THE LAST Byzantine Renaissance was essentially a Greek renaissance. But within its framework there were various vital controversial issues about which every thinking Byzantine had to make up his mind. It is dangerous to try to interpret Byzantine history in terms of party politics. In his political reactions the Byzantine followed the Greek tradition. The Greek has never been a good party politician. He is too individualistic. He will follow a leader whom he admires, though he is apt to find it boring to keep up admiration for any one person for long. He will co-operate with his friends so long as his interests coincide with theirs. Unless there have been family squabbles he will take proper trouble to ensure the advancement of his relatives. He does not regard consistency as one of the major virtues, nor does he like to look very far ahead. He is swayed by his individual opinions and prejudices, aspirations and interests, usually with an immediate end in view; and the end is by no means always materialistic.

In Byzantine times this individualism was tempered by a deep and genuine sense of religion. The Byzantine

Greek, unless he was seriously provoked, was loyal to the Empire and to the Emperor, because the Empire was the Christian Oecumene, the Kingdom of God on earth, and the Emperor was its holy symbol of authority, the viceroy of God. The loyalty was seldom given to the Emperor as a man, and it would be removed were the Emperor clearly unworthy of his sacred rôle. It was only on religious issues that there was anything that might be called party politics in Byzantium. There the need that the Byzantine felt to keep the Faith pure naturally bound him to such others as shared his views on what was the pure Faith. There he looked ahead; for his eternal life in the world to come was at stake.

There were factions, certainly. But the Circus factions of the sixth century, the Blues and the Greens, only became parties when they were caught up in the Monophysite controversy. The Iconoclastic controversy was over a religious issue. The struggle between the civil service and the landed aristocracy in the eleventh century was more purely political; but it was not party warfare so much as an attempt by the central government to control a baronage made up of a number of great families all bitterly jealous of each other. There was an administrative issue, in that the growth of the power of the baronage meant the break-up of the system on which taxation and military recruitment had been based. But small groups whose motive force was the

desire for personal or family aggrandizement can hardly
be called political parties. The civil wars of the fourteenth century were principally based on personal
ambition. Andronicus III and his friends fought
against Andronicus II not on any political grounds but
simply because the younger generation was impatient
of the old incompetent Emperor and his old incompetent ministers. John Cantacuzenus rebelled in 1341 not
because he disagreed with governmental policy but
because he had been outwitted by his former friend,
Alexius Apocaucus. Apocaucus was certainly able to
organize riots against Cantacuzenus's friends in Constantinople. But the city proletariat was always ready to
respond to any encouragement to pillage the houses
of the rich. It is absurd to call this a social movement
against the landed aristocracy when Apocaucus himself
and many of his friends belonged to the same class, and
their houses were unharmed. The same is true of the
riots similarly organized in Adrianople and other
Thracian towns, which had the effect of turning general
public opinion in Thrace in Cantacuzenus's favour. If
the Thessalian magnates supported Cantacuzenus, so
too, as far as we can tell, did the poorer Thessalians, as
he was very popular there, having been responsible in
the last reign for restoring Thessaly to the Empire. In
so far as there was a 'popular' party it was the party of
the religious Zealots, the successors of the Arsenites,
led by monks who moved about amongst the populace

and moulded opinion there. They were suspicious of the wealthy intellectuals of the Court of which John Cantacuzenus was a prominent example, and at first they seem to have been opposed to him, preferring the more demagogic Apocaucus and John Calecas. But they seem to have had little effect on the outcome of the civil war.[1]

The Zealot movement in Thessalonica was in a rather different position. It was more a local nationalist movement. The citizens of the great city, which was probably almost as populous as Constantinople and who were on an average richer than the Constantino-politans, resented being governed in the interests of the capital and the hierarchs and rich magnates of the countryside; and their resentment was expressed in massacres. But the Zealots were not anti-religious, much as they hated the hierarchy and the richer monasteries. The poorer monks were their friends and allies. It was not for nothing that the Religious Zealots and the Political Zealots shared the same name. They might disagree on Hesychasm; but neither had any use for intellectuals.[2]

The intellectuals could therefore unite in disapproving of the Zealot movement. But there were three main controversies on which they could disagree amongst themselves.

The first and oldest of these questions, which had

[1] See above, p. 11, n. 1.   [2] See above, p. 13, n. 1.

been debated since the triumph of Christianity, was not by now a source of much trouble. It was: how far could a scholar go along the path of ancient philosophy without endangering his Christian faith?[1]

Byzantium had always drawn a distinction between the Outer Learning, which was the whole of Hellenic secular learning, and the Inner Learning, which was Christian theology. Byzantine education was based on the old Hellenic system of the *trivium* and the *quadrivium*, which included elementary philosophy. When he had finished this regular course a student of ability could go on to study law or medicine or mathematics or higher philosophy at the University, or, if it were in abeyance, at the feet of some distinguished private teacher. But should the boy wish to enter the religious life, he passed from the Outer Learning to the Inner Learning, which was taught at some monastic or ecclesiastic institution and above all at the Patriarchal Academy. The Council *in Trullo* had ordained that only clerics should teach theology and that laymen should not be admitted into its mysteries.[2] The first of these ordinances was in general but not invariably obeyed.

[1] Dr D. M. Nicol has kindly allowed me to see, before publication, the text of his article on 'The Byzantine Church and Hellenic Learning in the Fourteenth Century,' published in *Studies in Church History*, v (Leiden, 1969), 23–57. He goes into the question in some detail. I am glad to find that his conclusions roughly coincide with mine.

[2] Council *in Trullo*, canon 64, in J. P. Migne, *Patrologia Graeco-Latina* (Paris, 1857–66), vol. CXXXVII, col. 736.

The second was impossible to enforce. Theological students did not always stay the course, while there were a number of lay intellectuals who did not intend to be deprived of the Inner Learning. Throughout Byzantine history there were laymen who were well trained in theology, having studied either at the Academy or some other school or under some eminent ecclesiastic. Indeed, some of the most learned of the Patriarchs, such as Photius, were laymen until the eve of their elevation but were already highly erudite theologians.

But there were always clerics who were suspicious of ancient learning. The *Didascalia of the Apostles* wished entirely to proscribe its study;[1] and Origen, for all his own excellent education, was doubtful of its value.[2] The biographer of Theodore the Studite apologized for his hero having received a full secular education.[3] The biographer of John the Psychaite, a few years later, dismisses Homer as a gas-bag and the sciences of astronomy, geometry and arithmetic as sciences of the non-existent.[4] Nicholas Stethatus in his panegyric of Symeon the New Theologian boasts that Symeon

---

[1] *Didascalia Apostolorum*, trans. M. D. Gibson (London, 1901), p. 101, recommending that education should be technical only.

[2] For Origen's rather equivocal views about Classical learning, see J. Tixeront, *Histoire des Dogmes* (Paris, 1930), I, 296–303.

[3] *Vita S. Theodori Studitae*, in Migne, *Patrologia Graeco-Latina*, vol. xcix, cols. 117–20.

[4] See G. da Costa-Louillet, 'Saints de Constantinople aux VIIIe, IXe et Xe siècles', *Byzantion*, xxiv (Brussels, 1954), 259.

had rejected learning, though the evidence of Symeon's writings suggests otherwise.[1] A few laymen shared these views, such as the old soldier Cecaumenus, who thought that it was enough for a boy to study the Bible, the Old Testament for strategy and the New Testament for morals, and a little logic.[2] But these anti-intellectuals, though they drew support from many of the monks, never commanded the main body of the Church organization. The most admired of the early Fathers of the Church, Clement of Alexandria, John Chrysostom, Maximus the Confessor or John of Damascus, had all been trained in the old Classical way and were proud of it; and it had been above all to the Cappadocian saints, Basil and his brother Gregory, that the survival of the Classical system was due.[3] This tradition lasted on, with bishops such as the saintly John Mauropus of Euchaita, who wrote an epigram asking Christ to receive Plato in heaven,[4] or Eustathius of Thessalonica, or Michael Acominatus of Athens.

But the question still remained: where was the fron-

[1] Nicetas Stethatos, *Vie de Symeon le Nouveau Théologien*, ed. I. Hausherr, *Orientalia Christiana*, XII (Rome, 1928), 4.
[2] Cecaumenus, *Strategicon*, ed. B. Wassiliewsky (St Petersburg, 1896), pp. 46, 75.
[3] For the early Fathers' approval of Classical learning, see W. Jaeger, *Early Christianity and Greek Paideia* (Cambridge, Mass., 1962), *passim*, esp. pp. 46 ff., 73 ff.
[4] Mauropus's poem is given in G. Soyter, *Byzantinische Dichtung* (Heidelberg, 1930), p. 26.

tier between the Outer and the Inner Learning? The sciences could be legitimately studied, for they attempted only to explain things that lay within the dimensions of the created universe. They did not exceed the bounds of the Outer Learning. But philosophy attempted to explain rather more. The general opinion seems to have been that the works of the ancient philosophers were valuable for training the mind. They could teach one how to think. But they could not teach one what to think. Theology, the Queen of the Sciences, was something apart. All that we could know of it was what had been revealed by God, in the Scriptures, in the inspired decisions of the Oecumenical Councils, in the works of the Saints of the Church and in the unwritten traditions handed down from the Apostles. Beyond that lay the mysteries that the human mind could not comprehend, about which all that we could know was that we knew nothing. This dominant apophatic element in Orthodox religion precluded any man-made explanation of eternal things. The philosophers could supply the technique that might enable our intellects to penetrate as far as the limits of the created and the revealed world. If we sought more from them we ran into danger.

Aristotle did not pose much of a problem, for he was mainly concerned in explaining the things of this world. Plato was different. His attitude was far more attractive to the Orthodox mind than was Aristotle's; and, indeed, since the days of Saint John the Divine, Platonism and

Neo-Platonism had played a large part in shaping Christian thought. Some revered writings, such as the works of the Pseudo-Areopagite, were almost purely Neo-Platonic. In unsophisticated circles Plato and Aristotle, with Plutarch not far behind, ranked with the prophets. You can see them painted in chapels on Mount Athos or on Orthodox churches in Moldavia.[1] But, in spite of John Mauropus's prayer, they were not Christians. Plato in particular was to be studied with caution. In the fourteenth century the mystical writer Gregory Palamas boasted of his training in Aristotelian logic but thanked God that he had not succumbed to the lure of Platonic philosophy.[2]

Nevertheless the Church, in spite of its anti-intellectual wing, was always shy of persecution. Intellectuals had been prosecuted in the ninth century, but that was because of the suspicion of Iconoclastic views. There had been a famous case in the mid-eleventh century when the celebrated Michael Psellus was deprived of his University Chair as Chief of the Philosophers for lecturing too enthusiastically on Platonic doctrines. But it must be remembered that he

[1] See *Mandeville's Travels*, ed. M. C. Seymour (Oxford, 1967), p. 12; F. W. Hasluck, *Christianity and Islam under the Sultans* (Oxford, 1929), II, 363–9; P. Henry, *Les Eglises de la Moldavie du Nord* (Paris, 1930), pp. 235–7, 274. The Tree of Jesse on the outside wall of churches such as Sucevitsa often includes Thucydides, Plutarch and even Porphyry.

[2] For Palamas's views on the philosophers, see J. Meyendorff, *Introduction à l'Etude de Grégoire Palamas* (Paris, 1959), pp. 45–50.

had many personal enemies who instigated the pro-
secution, as well as many personal friends who saw to it
that his career was not seriously damaged: also that he
was suspected of too great an interest in occultism, of
which the Church could not approve. Still more no-
torious was the case brought against his pupil John
Italus, who was in his turn deposed from the Chair of
Philosophy, and who ended his days obscurely in a
monastery. But here again there were personal elements
which are difficult to unravel. Italus was an Italian
Greek and as such suspect at a time when the Empire
was fighting desperately against the Norman rulers of
Southern Italy. He seems to have been a tactless man.
Moreover, it was the Emperor Alexius Comnenus
rather than the Church authorities, whose enmity he
seems to have aroused; and Alexius was anyhow not
fond of intellectuals, whatever his intellectual daughter
Anna may have pretended.[1]

These two prosecutions may have discouraged the
study of philosophy for a while. But philosophers were
teaching again at the University long before the end of
the twelfth century. Philosophy was accepted as a
legitimate branch of the Outer Learning; but it must
be the hand-maid of religion, and no substitute for it.

The scholars of the last Byzantine period were

[1] See Buckler, *Anna Comnena*, pp. 319–24; J. M. Hussey, *Church and Learning in the Byzantine Empire* (Oxford, 1937), pp. 73–95; P. E. Stephanou, *Jean Italos* (*Orientalia Christiana Analecta*, 134, Rome, 1949), *passim*.

brought up in this tradition and they kept to its rules, apparently without any conscious strain. When they argued about scientific matters, as did Metochites and Chumnus, they did so in secular terms based on Classical learning. When they argued about religious matters, about Hesychasm or union with Rome, they did so in religious terms. Even a scholar as well educated and as interested in the Classics as was Nicophorus Gregoras never overstepped the frontier. Only one Byzantine thinker of the period, George Gemistus Plethon, disobeyed the rules; and the work in which he aired un-Christian doctrines was never published. It is only from a few surviving fragments that we can see how shocking it would have appeared. Even so, Plethon's lectures might have invited trouble; but, on the advice of the Emperor Manuel II, he set up his school not in Constantinople but in the provincial capital of Mistra, where the Church authorities were less likely to interfere with him.

Had Plethon remained in Constantinople it might have been difficult for the authorities to have avoided taking action against him. This would have been embarrassing; for throughout the Palaeologan period the authorities in the Church hierarchy as well as in the State were men with a high regard for culture. The only Patriarch of the time who was not well educated was Michael VIII's appointee and subsequent opponent, Arsenius; and Arsenius, though his followers were most of them strongly anti-intellectual, opposed the government on a purely moral issue.[1] Even a protagonist of the mystical way of life such as Gregory Palamas took a Classical education for granted, though he disapproved of carrying it too far. Many of his followers, such as John Cantacuzenus and Nicholas Cabasilas, were in the forefront of the intellectual life of the time. The philosophers might seek new interpretations within the limits of philosophy, but they accepted its limits. They were in no danger of persecution, but they did nothing to invite it. They accepted the distinction between the Outer and the Inner Learning.

It was as well for them that they were at ease on this basic problem. For they had other bitter problems to face. Of these the most crucial and the most permanent was the question of the union of the Eastern Church with the Church of Rome. The problem involved politics as well as religion. The union was in many eyes politically desirable because it seemed to provide the only practical means for preserving the Empire itself, at first because it could be expected to ward off potential enemies from the West, and later, and even more urgently, because it might provide badly needed help against actual enemies from the East. But, though the government might stress the political advantages, the average Byzantine was only prepared to argue the question on religious grounds. His eyes were fixed on

---

[1] For Plethon, see below, pp. 77–9.

35

the next world. Political advantages were irrelevant if eternal salvation was to be endangered. He was conscious of the scandal of divided Christendom; he grieved that Christ's garment should be rent. But before he could contemplate the mending of the rent he needed assurances that his true Orthodox faith should not be compromised.

The schism between East and West had arisen from a number of causes; and, though neither side had wished for the breach to be irreparable, it had become absolute in the course of the twelfth century.[1] The religious differences fell under three headings. There was the theological issue of the Procession of the Holy Ghost, centring round the word *filioque* which the Latins had added to the Creed as it had been fixed at the Second Oecumenical Council. This was a matter that the Latins genuinely thought unimportant, the word merely clarifying their interpretation of the doctrine of the Trinity, but which to the Greeks could not be accepted, as the word contradicted their interpretation of the doctrine. In addition, its insertion seemed to them to be an insult to a Council inspired by the Holy Spirit. Then there were the liturgical differences, of which the chief were whether leavened or unleavened bread should be used at the Sacrament, the Greeks insisting on the

[1] It ought to be unnecessary by now to point out that the schism did not happen suddenly in 1054 but gradually developed. See S. Runciman, *The Eastern Schism* (Oxford, 1955), *passim*.

former and the Latins on the latter: and the Greek practice of the *epiklesis*, the prayer invoking the Holy Ghost at the consecration of the Host, a prayer which the Latins omitted. Finally, and most fundamentally, there was the ecclesiastical problem concerning the position of the Pope. The Patriarch of Constantinople and his Eastern fellow Patriarchs were prepared to give the Bishop of Rome the primacy of honour among the Patriarchs (so long as he would account for his heresy on the Procession of the Holy Ghost), but they would not accept that the primacy allowed him to meddle in their internal affairs and provide a court of appeal for their bishops: still less that it enabled him to pronounce on doctrine, which only an Oecumenical Council could do. If union with the Western Church involved submission to the dictates of the Roman pontiff, then the average Byzantine, layman and cleric alike, would not willingly agree to it. There were minor points of difference also, as over the doctrine of Purgatory or whether secular priests could marry, or with how many fingers and in which direction the sign of the Cross should be made. But the main quarrel was over the *filioque* clause, the question of the bread and the *epiklesis* and the Papal claim to ecclesiastical supremacy. In all of these items the Western view seemed to the East to be disrespectful to the Holy Spirit.[1]

---

[1] See S. Runciman, *The Great Church in Captivity* (Cambridge, 1968), pp. 86–96.

The schism had been embittered by the Fourth Crusade and the crude and clumsy attempts of the victorious Latins to force their form of religion on the Greeks. But could Byzantium afford to nurture a bitterness that united the West against it, at a time when Western power was growing and Byzantine power declining? Moreover, the scholars in Byzantium were beginning to realize that Western Europe, which they had for so long viewed with disdain, was now blossoming with cultural activity; and, as a result of the contact following the Latin conquest, Western scholars were just beginning to take an appreciative interest in Greek culture. Was it right to stand aside from this lively new world?

The Byzantine government had no wish to provoke unnecessary hostility. During the Nicaean period the Emperor John Vatatzes had carried on negotiations with the Papacy which at one moment seemed near to success. But Rome demanded conditions that seemed to the Byzantine clergy, who were anyhow far from enthusiastic about the union, too grossly humiliating; and the mistrust on both sides was too great.[1] Some of the scholars of the Court were, however, not unfavourable towards union. The learned Nicephorus Blemmydes hopefully suggested a formula dealing with the *filioque*, which was intended to satisfy the

[1] W. Norden, *Das Papsttum und Byzans* (Berlin, 1903), pp. 349 ff.

theologians on both sides. But neither side would accept it.[1]

A far more serious move towards union was that made by Michael VIII, in his attempt to counter the vengeful plans of Charles of Anjou by submitting to Charles's suzerain, the Pope. After long negotiations Michael sent delegates to the Council of Lyons in 1274, where they accepted in his name both Papal supremacy and the lawfulness of Roman theology. The Union of Lyons was ill-received at Constantinople. The delegates had been of no distinction theologically and did not represent the feeling of the Church; and only one was of intellectual distinction, the Emperor's secretary, the layman George Acropolites. The populace, to whom memories of persecution during the Latin Empire were still vivid, refused to accept it, backed by the vast majority of the clergy. There was opposition even in the Emperor's own family, led by his sister Eulogia and supported by his son Andronicus. Michael attempted to use penal measures to enforce the union; but that merely roused stronger hostility to Rome. On Mount Athos legends of Michael's persecution were more numerous and more horrifying than legends of persecutions under the Latin Empire. The Papacy grew impatient at the Emperor's failure to implement the union, and refused to give him help.

[1] M. Jugie, *Theologia Dogmatica Christianorum Orientalium ab Ecclesia Catholica Dissidentium* (5 vols., Paris, 1926–35), I, 417–18.

4-2

The Empire was saved from Charles of Anjou not by Papal intervention but by the massacre of the Sicilian Vespers.[1]

Michael considered himself nevertheless bound by the union; and he was supported not only by his secretary Acropolites but also by the eminent theologian whom he had appointed Patriarch, John Beccus. Beccus had been influenced by a Franciscan of Greek origin, John Parastron, who lived as Papal legate at Constantinople and whose personal charm impressed even his opponents. Under his guidance Beccus and his rather less distinguished pupils, Constantine of Melitene and George Metochites, wrote well-thought-out tracts in favour of Roman doctrines. But they made few converts.[2] When Michael VIII died Andronicus II repudiated the Union of Lyons and replaced Beccus by the scholar George of Cyprus, who became the Patriarch Gregory II. George and his friends were not as bitter against the union as many of their compatriots. They disliked the idea of Papal supremacy, but they were eager to find a formula that would satisfy both sides of the *filioque* controversy. The historian George Pachymer suggested that though the word *filioque* was unjustified it might be admitted that the Son did have some part in the Procession of the Holy Ghost. George

[1] See D. J. Geanakoplos, *Emperor Michael Palaeologus and the West* (Cambridge, Mass., 1952), pp. 258 ff.

[2] *Ibid.* pp. 267–8 (for Parastron), and 307–9; Jugie, *Theologia Dogmatica*, I, 418–22.

of Cyprus himself put forward a formula that he hoped would be acceptable. But, as Beccus unkindly pointed out, it depended on there being a distinction between 'existing' and 'being in existence'. It, and all other such formulae, pleased no one but their inventors.[1]

When in the course of the fourteenth century the Turkish menace became ominous, the Byzantine government thought again of union. The help of the Western powers was needed; but they would not come to help a schismatic Empire. John VI Cantacuzenus tried to open negotiations; but nothing came of them. In 1355 the Emperor John V, the son of a Latin mother, offered to submit to Rome if the Pope would send him five galleys, a thousand foot-soldiers and five hundred horsemen. On those terms he would, he said, be able to convert all his subjects within six months, and he would send his second son, Manuel, to Italy for his education; and he undertook to abdicate in Manuel's favour should he not himself achieve the union. But the Pope had no troops to send. A Papal legate armed only with the Papal blessing was an inadequate substitute. Fourteen years later, when on a visit to Italy, John made his personal submission

---

[1] George of Cyprus's views, including the distinction between ὑπάρχει and ὕπαρξιν ἔχει, are given in Migne, *Patrologia Graeco-Latina*, vol. CXLII, cols. 233–46; and Beccus's rejoinder in *ibid.* vol. CXLI, cols. 896–924. See Jugie, *Theologia Dogmatica*, I, 429–31; Beck, *Kirche und theologische Literatur*, pp. 685–6.

to the Pope at Rome; but he would not involve his subjects.[1]

The bulk of these subjects remained hostile to any arrangement with Rome. But in intellectual circles there was a growing interest in Western culture. A number of Western scholars began to visit Constantinople where many of them made an excellent impression. Soon Greek scholars were being invited to Italy and offered Chairs there. Translations from Latin into Greek began to appear; and when in about 1360 the young Demetrius Cydones published a Greek version of the *Summa contra Gentiles* of Thomas Aquinas, the distinguished, if restricted, group that read the work was deeply impressed. In such circles it seemed ridiculous not to make an effort to come together religiously with their brilliant Italian friends.[2]

The problem could not now be ignored. It was hoped that an Oecumenical Council whose decisions the Eastern Churches would respect might be able to resolve the difficulties. But Rome declared that the Council of Lyons had been oecumenical, and none other was needed. The Conciliar movement in the West resulted in a modification of the Roman position. But if a new Council was to be held, where should it meet? The Greeks were afraid of being outnumbered

[1] Norden, *Das Papsttum und Byzans*, pp. 696–711; G. Ostrogorsky, *History of the Byzantine State*, trans. J. M. Hussey (Oxford, 1956), pp. 476–81.
[2] See below, pp. 74–5.

and browbeaten were it to be held in the West. The Latins were not prepared to come to the doomed city of Constantinople, where, too, they in their turn would probably be outnumbered.[1] The Emperor Manuel II, who was interested in Western culture, was eager to create good-will and hoped that something might come out of the Conciliar movement; he sent an observer to the Council of Basle. But he did not want to go too far, both because he was not going to yield on theological points and because he knew that his people hated the idea of actual union. His policy was to negotiate but never to commit himself.[2] But his son, John VIII, was desperate in his need for aid. After long negotiations a Council was arranged which met at Ferrara in 1438 and was soon transferred to Florence. The Union was signed in July 1439. Though the Byzantine delegation had included most of the leading theologians and philosophers of the time, and though only one member flatly refused to sign the Union decree, which gave the Roman Church all that it had demanded, apart from a doubtfully worded formula on Papal supremacy, once again the people of Constantinople, led by many of the bishops and all the lower clergy, refused to accept it. The government was powerless to enforce it: though eventually the Union decree was read out in Saint

[1] See J. Gill, *The Council of Florence* (Cambridge, 1959), pp. 16 ff.
[2] *Ibid.* pp. 46 ff. For Manuel's advice to his son on union, see G. Phrantzes (Sphrantzes), *Chronicon*, ed. I Bekker (Bonn, 1838), p. 178.

Sophia in the winter of 1452, at a ceremony almost entirely boycotted by the Greeks. Little was gained from it. There was one great expedition that perished at the hands of the Turks at Varna. There was a gallant handful of Westerners who came to support the Empire in its final agony. But the main result of the Union of Florence was to bring dispute and bitterness to the dying Empire. It was only when the actual siege of the city by the Turks began that Unionists and non-Unionists would work whole-heartedly together again.

The polemical writings on the schism and the debates at the Union Councils make sterile reading. The same arguments recur, and the same misunderstandings, made worse by the difficulty of translating theological terms. There were endless references to the works of the Fathers of the Church, but with differing interpretations; and the Fathers themselves were not always consistent with each other or even with themselves. The Greek and Latin versions of Conciliar acts often differed. There was a profound difference between the outlook of Greek traditional theology and the Latin theology of the time, though the Latins tried to minimize it and many Greek scholars were attracted by the Latin attitude. At the Council of Florence the Latins who worked as a team outclassed the Greeks who argued as individuals. The political side of the question, which must have been in everyone's mind, was barely mentioned until the final crisis. The cultural side was only suggested rather than stated in the arguments. True to their traditions the Byzantine scholars had to justify their varying views on theological grounds.[1]

One other great controversy agitated the minds of Greek scholars in the fourteenth century. It was over the nature of mysticism. There had always been a strong mystical element in the Byzantine Church. The mystical writings of Gregory of Nazianzus, of John Climacus, of the Pseudo-Areopagite and of others in their tradition had always been read and admired. In the early eleventh century, Symeon the New Theologian had given new force to the tradition; and by the end of the thirteenth century mystical practices were widespread in Byzantine monasteries, especially on Mount Athos, and were even followed in sophisticated circles in Constantinople. The mystics, the Hesychasts, or Quietists, as they were usually called, believed that through intense contemplation, for which certain exercises provide a helpful prelude, they could rise to a state of mystical ecstasy in which they could make contact with the divine.

As in so many aspects of Orthodox faith, which, in its apophatic modesty, dislikes hard theological definitions, the theological theory of mysticism had never been clearly stated because it had never been questioned. But by the fourteenth century there was a

[1] The discussions at Florence are fully given in Gill, *Council of Florence*, pp. 131 ff.

45

growing feeling among many intellectuals that the mystical practices of the Hesychasts were barely Christian. These views were given expression by a Calabrian Greek, Barlaam, who had succeeded in quarrelling with a number of Byzantine scholars on other philosophical and religious grounds. Amongst his opponents was a learned monk, Gregory Palamas, who wrote courteously to him to criticize his doctrine of the Incarnation. Barlaam was furious, and, knowing Palamas to sympathize with the Hesychasts, made it his business to refute their doctrines and ridicule their practices. He delightedly discovered a group of Hesychast monks in Thessalonica who claimed to attain to the divine vision by gazing concentratedly at their navels. He made great fun of them, and then went on to ask how indeed could any mystic see God Who is invisible.[1]

Palamas's reply was fully given in a great work which he called *Triads in Defence of the Holy Hesychasts*. In it, while he defended the use of exercises and saw nothing wrong with navel-gazing as a possible aid to contemplation, his main object was to prove that what the mystics could perceive, if they attained so far, was not God Himself, but His uncreated energies. What could be experienced at the summit of mystical experience was the Light of God, the Light that had shone on Mount Thabor at the Transfiguration of Our Lord, the light

---

[1] For the whole history and circumstances of the Palamite controversy see Meyendorff, *Introduction à...Grégoire Palamas, passim.*

which the Byzantines suggested by the mandorla, the rays that surround Christ in glory. The light was an Energy of God, to be distinguished from His Essence, which is invisible and indivisible. This was not a new doctrine. It was inherent in the works of the Cappadocian Fathers, though they preferred the word 'powers' to 'energies', and of Maximus the Confessor and John of Damascus. But it had never before been clearly stated, because it had never been definitely challenged. To many of the philosophers of the fourteenth century, however, men less well grounded in the works of the Christian Fathers and, some of them, affected by Western scholasticism, it seemed new and unacceptable. If the Light is God, it must be of His Essence and therefore inseparable from Him. They could not allow a distinction between Essence and Energy.[1]

This is not the place for a deep discussion of the theological arguments. In the outcome Palamism triumphed, partly because it had the approval of the majority of the Greek clergy, partly because it had the political support of John Cantacuzenus, and partly because of the personality and intellect of Palamas himself. The doctrine of the Energies was endorsed by a Council of the Eastern Churches in 1351, and since then it has been an article of Orthodox belief. But it had been bit-

[1] The *Triads* have been edited and published with a French translation by J. Meyendorff; see Grégoire Palamas, *Défense des Saints Hésychastes* (2 vols., Louvain, 1959). Palamas's other published works can be found in Migne, *Patrologia Graeco-Latina*, vol. CL.

terly opposed by scholars of the calibre of Nicephorus Gregoras, George Akyndinus and Demetrius Cydones. It was denounced as being heretical by Rome and so became an added cause for contention between the Eastern and Western Churches. At the Council of Florence the Emperor, in his desire to avoid further controversy, forbade an attempt to raise the question. But, as we shall see, the anti–Palamites were not all of them in favour of union with Rome, nor were they all politically opposed to John Cantacuzenus. In his controversies the individual Greek scholar pursued in all sincerity his own individual course. He might belong to a faction, but never to a party.

3

THE SCHOLARS

IN THESE modern days when a sharp line is drawn between the humanities and the sciences it is a relief to look back to an age when a cultured man was expected to take an interest in all branches of human knowledge. The 'complete man' of the Italian Renaissance represented an ideal that only a Michelangelo or a Leonardo could reach. But he was foreshadowed by Western medieval scholars such as Roger Bacon, and by the best scholars of Byzantium, especially during the last two centuries of the Christian Empire.

There was a gap in the completeness. The Byzantine scholars made no attempts to be painters or sculptors. Practising artists did not enjoy a high status in Byzantium, great as was the Byzantine devotion to art. Except for a few manuscript miniaturists and a few fresco-painters working on the perimeter of the Byzantine world, scarcely one Byzantine artist is known to us by name, and only one architect, the Armenian Tirdat, since the days of Justinian; and the great architects of Justinian's time, Anthemius of Tralles and Isidore of Miletus, and Isidore's nephew and namesake, the architects of Saint Sophia, were more renowned as geometricians than as the designers of buildings. In the ninth century Photius could describe the New Basilica of the Emperor Basil I without any mention of its architect or its decorators. This was largely because the Byzantine never thought in terms of individual works of art. A picture or a carving was to be seen in its setting, as part of a whole; and the whole was the product of a team. A church would have its architects, or 'geometricians', who calculated the dimensions of the building and its stresses, the builders, or 'architects', who carried out the structural work, the master-painters who drew the designs for the mosaics or the frescoes and the artisans who inserted the mosaic cubes or applied the paint, the specialists who chose and placed the marble slabs and the bas-reliefs and the artisans who were under their orders. The design was dictated by the purpose of the building; and the unifying force behind it was the patron who ordered and paid for the work. This corresponded with the Byzantine theory based on a curious interpretation of a passage in Aristotle's *Metaphysics*. A picture had several 'causes'. The most important was the 'formal' cause, which meant the prototype that the work represented—if an icon, Christ or the particular saint: if a church building, God's universe, of which it was a microcosm. Next was the 'poetic' cause, which was the patron who was responsible for commissioning the work and who was thus its ultimate maker. The 'organic' cause seems to have been the artist or craftsman, and the 'material' cause the actual material that he used. There was also the 'final' cause, which may have been the intended function of the work, or the need that it was required to fill, or may perhaps simply have been the finished work itself.[1]

The artist was thus considered to be a craftsman, and was kept in his place. A man of culture might perhaps, like the Emperor Constantine Porphyrogenitus, enjoy trying his hand at amateur painting;[2] but his proper function was to be the 'poetic' cause. Unfortunately it is not cheap to commission works of art, and artists are seldom wealthy men. Moreover wealth was growing scarce during the political decline of the Empire. The usual 'poetic' cause was the Imperial government or a member of the Imperial family. Around the beginning of the fourteenth century we find rich scholar–statesmen, such as Theodore Metochites and Nicephorus Chumnus, commissioning the decoration of whole churches. Later in the century, though the Despots of Mistra or the Emperors of Trebizond and their wealthier magnates might arrange for the frescoing of some smallish church, at Constantinople itself

---

[1] For theories of art and the rôle of the artist in Byzantium, see G. Mathew, *Byzantine Aesthetics* (London, 1963), esp. pp. 119–21.

[2] According to the Western ambassador Liudprand, Constantine VII was kept so short of money by his father-in-law and senior colleague, Romanus Lecapenus, that he painted pictures to make a living. Liudprand, *Opera*, ed. J. Becker (Hanover–Leipzig, 1915), pp. 91–2.

a patron could do little more than order an occasional illuminated manuscript. At the same time the substitution of the costly mosaic by the fresco, a substitution in which taste as well as economy probably played a part, and by the icon painted on wood led to the upgrading of the artist's position. A single artist could now design and execute the painted decoration of a whole church; and he began to record his name while doing so. Portable icons became more fashionable, and certain icon-painters began to be preferred to others less gifted. By the time that we reach the post-Byzantine period, artists' names are often and increasingly known.[1]

The practice of the arts was not the scholar's business. But he was expected to cover all other branches of culture. There were certainly amongst them men who specialized for choice in one branch only. For instance, all that we know of the work of Nicholas Rhabdas is contained in two remarkable letters, written in about 1350, which are purely concerned with mathematical and logistical problems. It is probable that he had no other interests.[2] Gregory Choniades, who died in Constantinople in about 1300 after having founded an academy at Trebizond for the study of astronomy,

---

[1] The first Byzantine fresco-artists to sign their names seem to have been Greeks working in Serbia. The only miniature painters whose signatures we have are the eight who worked on Basil II's *Menologion*.

[2] For Rhabdas, see G. Sarton, *Introduction to the History of Science* (Baltimore, 1927–48), III, part 1, 681–2.

never, as far as we know, wrote on any other subject, though he taught himself Persian and Arabic in the pursuit of his studies. The same is true of Manuel of Trebizond, who taught at this academy. On the other hand, Manuel's pupil, George Chrysococces, wrote on medicine and geography as well as on astronomy.[1] Triclinius, the great commentator on Classical literature, whose work was much admired in his own time and still is important today, seems never to have departed from his chosen sphere.[2] The division between the Inner and the Outer Learning meant that theologians, such as Gregory Palamas, would not have thought of writing on the sciences; and lesser devotees of the Inner Learning, such as George Moschampus or the Patriarch John Beccus, never ventured outside theology.

There was, however, no merit in being a specialist. The sciences overlapped, and all were part of philosophy in the fullest sense of the word. Even the Queen of the Sciences, theology, could make use of philosophy in so far as it concerned itself with human reason and the things of the created world. The traditional education system of the *trivium* and the *quadrivium* aimed at providing a general knowledge of the Outer

---

[1] See *ibid.* pp. 688–90. For a fuller account of these astronomers, see D. Pingree, 'Gregory Choniades and Palaeologan Astronomy', *Dumbarton Oaks Papers*, no. 18 (Washington, 1964), pp. 133–60.

[2] Krumbacher, *Byzantinischen Litteratur*, pp. 554–5. Krumbacher considered Triclinius to be on a level with most modern editors of the Classics.

Learning; and the higher education provided by the University, while for practical purposes it might concentrate on law and medicine, covered the whole range of philosophy as well. The University had been in abeyance during the exile at Nicaea. It was refounded by Michael VIII soon after his recovery of Constantinople and was situated in the outbuildings of Saint Sophia, conveniently under the Patriarch's eye. Its first head, George Acropolites, lectured on mathematics as well as on pure philosophy. His main courses were on Euclid and Nicomachus and on Aristotle.[1] Andronicus II, apparently on the advice of his Grand Logothete, enlarged the University and placed it under the Grand Logothete's care. Professors' salaries were paid by the State, but, as an innovation, parents had to provide a small sum to supplement them.[2] During the troubles of the fourteenth century the University seems to have declined, probably from lack of public funds; and the best higher education was provided by private schools such as that run by Nicephorus Gregoras at the monastery of the Chora.[3] Such schools probably had some connection with the skeleton organization maintained at the University. At the end of the century Manuel II re-organized higher education. He moved the University to the monastery of Saint John in

[1] F. Fuchs, *Die Höheren Schulen von Konstantinopel im Mittelalter* (Leipzig, 1926), pp. 54–8.

[2] *Ibid.* pp. 62–5.

[3] R. Guilland, *Essai sur Nicéphore Grégoras* (Paris, 1926), pp. 13–14.

Petrion, where there was a good library which students could use. At the same time he placed the Patriarchal Academy in the monastery of Saint John in Studion, where, too, the library was good. The University, now called the *Catholicon Mouseion*, was put under one of the four Judges-General. It seems to have shared professors with the Patriarchal Academy. Both institutions were active till the fall of the city.[1]

The germs of this new comprehensive learning were developing in the twelfth century; but it was at the Nicaean Court that it began to blossom, under the influence of Nicephorus Blemmydes. He was the perfect polymath. He was born in about 1197, the son of a physician. After studying medicine and philosophy at Smyrna he went to sit at the feet of a hermit monk in Bithynia, called Prodromus, from whom he learnt mathematics and astronomy. He then settled in Nicaea where he studied theology. The Emperor John Vatazes thought highly of him and encouraged him to found a school, where his pupils included the heir to the throne, Theodore, and George Acropolites. In 1235 he retired to a monastery at Scamandros, but used at times to leave it to tour the Greek world in search of manuscripts scattered at the time of the Latin sack of Constantinople. In 1248 he founded his own monastery

[1] L. Bréhier, *Le Monde Byzantin* (3 vols., Paris, 1947–50), vol. III, *La Civilisation Byzantine*, pp. 484–97; Fuchs, *Die Höheren Schulen von Konstantinopel*, pp. 72–6.

at Ephesus, which remained his home until his death in 1272; but he paid several visits to the Imperial Court in the vain hope of being appointed Patriarch. He claimed that his former pupil, Theodore II, had offered him the post but that he had been obliged to refuse, as the Emperor would not promise him sufficient freedom of action. The truth seems to have been that Theodore turned down his insistent demand to be appointed, knowing too well the defects in his character. The range of his writing was enormous. He wrote a handbook on logic and on physics, a geographical synopsis, a treatise on kingship, in order that Theodore II should learn to appreciate the value of philosophers, some poetry, several theological commentaries as well as his treatise on the Holy Ghost, which was intended to satisfy both Greeks and Latins by showing that the Holy Ghost proceeded from the Father and the Son, but principally from the Father—thereby pleasing nobody, as it clearly showed that he understood neither the Greek nor the Latin doctrine—and an autobiography in two parts, a work full of fascinating detail but almost unreadable, as his style is amongst the most ornate and long-winded in all Byzantine literary history. He was a vain, self-righteous, ill-tempered and vindictive man; but his love of learning was genuine and his erudition immense.[1]

[1] For Blemmydes and his works, see Krumbacher, *Byzantinischen Litteratur*, pp. 445–9; Beck, *Kirche und theologische Literatur*, pp.

Of his two most distinguished pupils, the Emperor Theodore II wrote on philosophy, his main work being *Six Books on the Unity of Nature*, and a book called *The Explanation of the Universe*, written after his ascension to the throne. It is a curious production, consisting largely of apologies for his inadequate knowledge of the sciences. Probably it was intended to be taken ironically, as an attempt to ridicule the vaunted polymathy of his old tutor. Unfortunately he had learnt from his old tutor a literary style almost as verbose as Blemmydes's own; and it is sometimes quite impossible to follow his language or his thought. This is to be regretted, as he had an original mind and tried to re-assess the teachings of the ancient philosophers and to reinforce them by his own ideas. His distinction between *natura naturans* and *natura naturata* brings him nearer in thought to Spinoza than to any philosopher of the past.[1]

George Acropolites was a little older than Theodore and had succeeded Blemmydes as Theodore's tutor. He was a gentle, lovable man, who managed, however, to arouse Theodore's displeasure and whose subsequent support of Michael VIII's usurpation was ethically hard to defend. His political career as Michael's secretary was not very happy, though he seems to have

671–3; Gardner, *Lascarids of Nicaea*, pp. 278–82; B. Tatakis, *La Philosophie Byzantine* (Paris, 1949: fasciscule supplémentaire no. II of E. Bréhier, *Histoire de la Philosophie*), pp. 223–5.

[1] Gardner, *Lascarids of Nicaea*, pp. 197–211, 286–90; Tatakis, *Philosophie Byzantine*, pp. 235–9.

enjoyed his visit as a delegate to the Council of Lyons. He was an excellent and popular head of the restored University of Constantinople. His learning was wide; but his only important literary work was his *Chronicle*, a history of his own times, which is well written and full of invaluable information, but not unprejudiced nor always strictly accurate. His two theological works were composed to justify the Latin doctrine of the Procession of the Holy Ghost. His prose shows a welcome move towards a simpler style. He also wrote an amount of ceremonial poetry, and, it seems, like most Byzantine scholars, a vast number of letters; but none has survived.[1]

Amongst Acropolites's pupils at the University was George of Cyprus. He escaped as a boy from his native island where, under Frankish rule, a Greek could not obtain any higher education, and he planned to go to Ephesus to study under Blemmydes. When he was told of the old gentleman's cantankerous temperament he changed his mind and went on to seek Acropolites, whom he found just settled in Constantinople. George, who later became the Patriarch Gregory II, was not, as we have noticed, very successful in his theological writing, but he wrote sensibly if unoriginally on geometry and geography, and produced an attractive short autobiography.[2]

---

[1] Gardner, *Lascarids of Nicaea*, pp. 282–6; Beck, *Kirche und theologische Literatur*, pp. 674–5.

[2] See above, pp. 40–1. The text of the autobiography is given in Migne, *Patrologia Graeco-Latina*, vol. 142, cols. 19–30.

A more distinguished pupil of Acropolites was George Pachymer, who was born in 1242 and died in 1310. His best-known work is his history of his own times, which is amongst the finest productions of Byzantine historiography. It is slightly marred by a determination, characteristic of the time, to find the correct Attic term for every name that he uses, whether of nations or even of the months; but it is reliable and fair-minded. Pachymer was a deacon of the Church and for a time a professor at the Patriarchal Academy. He wrote a little on theology, as when he sought to find a compromise formula on the *filioque* dispute, and long works on philosophy which have never been printed, as well as a useful handbook on the *quadrivium*; but his main interest was in mathematics and the theory of music. He understood though he did not employ Arabic numerals.[1]

Still more remarkable for the range of his erudition was the monk Maximus Planudes, who was born in 1260 and died in 1310. He was mainly self-taught, though he may have sat under George of Cyprus. He never held a University post but taught at a monastic school with which George had been connected. He was a good mathematician, who recommended the use of Arabic numerals. He wrote a historical geography. But his fame rested on his philological and grammatical

[1] Tatakis, *Philosophie Byzantine*, pp. 239–40; Sarton, *History of Science*, II, part 2, 972–3.

work. He wrote commentaries on Theocritus and Hermogenes. He compiled an anthology of epigrams, and dabbled himself in poetry. He re-wrote Aesop's *Fables*. More remarkably, he learnt Latin. He was not the first Byzantine scholar to do so. Byzantine lawyers had always acquired a smattering of Latin; and Manuel Holobolus, who was about twenty years older than Planudes, had made a serious study of the language. But Planudes actually translated Latin works into Greek. His translations included extracts from Ovid and from Cicero, Boethius's *Consolation of Philosophy* and Saint Augustine's work on the Trinity. He was not always a very accurate translator, but he captured something of the feeling of the original. He had at first favoured the union of the Churches, as he showed in his translation of Augustine's work. After Andronicus II's succession he changed his mind and wrote against the Latin doctrine of the *filioque*. The change was probably sincere. Unlike most Byzantine scholars he seems to have lacked political ambition. His only public post, that of ambassador to Venice in 1297, brought him no satisfaction.[1]

It should be noted that these philosopher-scientists were nearly all of them involved in the Church organization. Blemmydes and Planudes were monks, Pachy-

[1] Tatakis, *Philosophie Byzantine*, pp. 240–3; Sarton, *History of Science*, II, part 2, 973–4; Krumbacher, *Byzantinischen Litteratur*, pp. 543–6; Fuchs, *Die Höheren Schulen von Konstantinopel*, pp. 58–62.

mer a deacon. Acropolites, though he remained a layman, was an accepted theologian. George of Cyprus rose to be Patriarch. Outside of Arsenite circles the Outer Learning and Inner Learning worked in harmony. It was only the Roman question that roused controversy, owing to Michael VIII's fierce attempts to implement the union that his delegates had signed at Lyons. Scholars who supported the union, such as Acropolites and George Metochites, found themselves cold-shouldered by their former friends.[1] As the fourteenth century advanced this controversy died down. Negotiations continued, and men still argued on the question. But there was no actual attempt to enforce union on the Byzantines. That was to take place in the next century, and then the bitterness would be revived. In the meantime, though scholars might discuss the merits and demerits of union, the debates did not break up friendships or ruin careers. It was the Palamite controversy that was to play that rôle.

It is not possible in a short study to list all the Byzantine scholars of the fourteenth century. We can only glance at the careers of the more significant of them. In the restricted world that Byzantium had now become, these scholars were all acquainted with each other, even if they did not all like each other. They corresponded with each other, sometimes cordially and sometimes with animosity. The Imperial Court con-

[1] See Geanakoplos, *Emperor Michael Palaeologos*, pp. 273 ff.

sistently patronized scholarship; so most of them gravitated there and intrigued to secure posts or influence there. There was at first a second centre of scholarship at Thessalonica. But it was dispersed after the Zealot rising in the 1340s; and even before the rising the Thessalonians liked to be in touch with Constantinople, and many of them settled there.[1] Trebizond had its schools and its renowned astronomical academy; but bright young Trapezuntines preferred to come to Constantinople. Scholars might retire now and then to Mount Athos or to monasteries elsewhere in search of quiet; but controversy often followed them there. The scholars formed a society that was at the same time closely knit, highly individualistic, jealous and quarrelsome, but ready as never before in Byzantine history to look at traditional thought with a fresh critical eye.

The chief patrons of the new generation of scholars were the two leading ministers of the pious and cultured Andronicus II. Nicephorus Chumnus and Theodore Metochites had remarkably similar careers. Each came to the Court as a young man. Each was chief magistrate at Thessalonica before attaining to high office in Constantinople. Each married a daughter into the Imperial family and so entered the inner ring of the Byzantine aristocracy. Each was a 'poietes' of art, endowing, rebuilding and decorating a great monastery. Each encouraged young scholars and found time to

[1] See above, p. 20.

write a vast number of books and letters; and each, perhaps because of these distractions, proved to be an ineffectual administrator. Each remained devotedly loyal to Andronicus II, though Chumnus predeceased him. Each retired into a monastery. For much of their careers they were good friends, but eventually embarked on a fierce intellectual controversy, though, courteously, neither mentioned the other's name in his polemical tracts.

Chumnus was slightly the elder. He was born at Thessalonica in about 1260 and always retained a deep affection for his native city. He studied at Constantinople under George of Cyprus. He wrote on philosophy, his tastes being Aristotelian but tempered by an overriding sense of apophatic theology. He was interested in natural science, particularly in meteorology; and he particularly concerned himself with rhetoric and style. He advocated clarity, simplicity and brevity in writing, but did not always practise those virtues. He was a haughty, touchy man, not much liked outside of his immediate circle. Of the monastery that he beautified, Our Lady of Prompt Succour, nothing remains.[1]

Theodore Metochites was some ten years younger than Chumnus. His father was George Metochites,

[1] For Chumnus, see J. Verpeaux, *Nicéphore Choumnos, Homme d'état et Humaniste Byzantin* (Paris, 1959), *passim*; and I. Ševčenko, *Études sur la Polémique entre Théodore Métochite et Nicéphore Choumnos* (Brussels, 1962), *passim*.

who had been one of the few scholarly supporters of the Union of Lyons and had therefore fallen into disgrace with Andronicus II. But though Theodore started his career under this cloud, he soon won the Emperor's confidence and affection. He became Grand Logothete in 1320 and remained the Emperor's loyal helper to the last. On the old man's dethronement he retired to his monastery of the Chora. His erudition was immense; and he wrote on every branch of the Outer Learning. Perhaps because of his family background he avoided theology, though he composed one or two hagiographical studies. He wrote funeral orations and eulogies, both in prose and in verse, besides numerous works on philosophy, education and the sciences. He was especially proud of his knowledge of astronomy, to which he came late in life, having at last found a worthy teacher in the mathematician Michael Bryennius. He thought highly of the importance of history; and his commentaries show an honest objectivity, not only as regards the Classical period but also as regards later periods. His most celebrated work was his *Miscellanea*, a collection of 120 essays on philosophy and politics, which is impregnated by his knowledge of the Classics and his preference for Plato to Aristotle and by his readiness to think things out for himself. His controversy with Chumnus opened on the question of style, over which it is difficult not to sympathize with Chumnus; for Metochites was one of those Byzantine writers who never used one word if ten would suffice. The argument then moved into the sphere of philosophy and the rival merits of Aristotle and Plato. Here Metochites with his larger scholarship and his finer understanding of the ancients emerged the victor. He was not, in fact, a very profound thinker, and his verbosity often obscures his meaning. He was also a trifle chauvinistic, refusing, for instance, to take any interest in Arabic numerals, as the Greeks had no need for new-fangled foreign inventions, though he admitted that they had learnt from older nations in the past. But the extent and accuracy of his erudition, backed by a stupendous memory, and the freshness of his approach thrilled the students that sat at his feet and made him a powerful influence for enlightenment. The mosaics and frescoes of the church of Saint Saviour in Chora remain as a testimony to his piety and his taste.[1]

At Thessalonica, where the influence of Eustathius lasted on and where Triclinius had been brought up, the master whom young students revered was a friend of both these scholar-statesmen, but a man whose career was very different from theirs. Joseph the Philosopher, who lived from 1280 to 1330, was a monk who was happiest when he could lead the contemplative

[1] For Metochites, see H.-G. Beck, *Theodoros Metochites* (Munich, 1952), *passim*; Ševčenko, *Etudes sur la Polémique*, *passim*; H. Hunger, 'Theodoros Metochites als Vorlaufer des Humanismus in Byzanz', in *Byzantinische Zeitschrift*, XLV (Munich, 1952), 4–19; Tatakis, *Philosophie Byzantine*, pp. 249–56 (see below, p. 94, n. 1).

life. He had no worldly ambition and firmly refused the offer of the Patriarchate. But he believed in the value of a Classical education, and he prepared a vast encyclopedia, intended to correlate the various branches of Classical learning and to show how their interconnection and their understanding could help in the higher study of theology. His attitude to the Outer and the Inner Learning was followed by several later Thessalonians, in particular by Nicholas Cabasilas.[1]

At the capital Metochites's rôle as patron of scholarship was taken on by John Cantacuzenus, Grand Logothete under Andronicus III, later a rebel, then Emperor, and finally the monk Josaphat, who, like Metochites, was a man of wide learning himself. He was perhaps too much of an opportunist to be a great Emperor, and his rebellion had done infinite harm to the Empire. But he had an attractive personality and was loved by his friends and respected by his enemies. After his fall from power he was frequently invited to emerge from his retirement to play the rôle of elder statesman. His chief literary work was his History of his times, written during his retirement. Despite its length it is perhaps the most readable of all Byzantine histories. Its language is clear and straightforward, though he was overfond of echoing Thucydides. Though it is

[1] See M. Treu, 'Der Philosoph Joseph', in *Byzantinische Zeitschrift*, VIII (Munich, 1899), 1–64; Tatakis, *Philosophie Byzantine*, pp. 244–6; *Correspondence de Nicéphore Grégoras*, ed. Guilland, pp. 338–42.

not quite as impartial as he claimed, it is not unfair to his opponents, and its factual information is fairly reliable. Cantacuzenus's model for the history seems to have been Caesar's *Gallic Wars*, which he certainly had studied. He may therefore have known Latin; but there was already in existence a Greek translation of the *Gallic Wars*, which used to be thought, incorrectly, to be the work of Planudes. Cantacuzenus seems not to have written on the sciences, but he produced a number of theological works, Christian apologias directed against the Jews and against the Muslims, and tracts in favour of Palamite doctrines, in which he devoutly believed. It was only against the opponents of Palamism that he felt any hostility, even imprisoning, though without severity, his old friend Gregoras. His attitude towards Rome was friendly, though he was careful not to commit himself to any scheme for union. Demetrius Cydones, the strongest advocate of union amongst the scholars of the time and a convinced opponent of Palamism, remained one of his closest friends. But Cydones, unlike Gregoras, was not a vain and quarrelsome man.[1]

Of all the Byzantine polymaths, Nicephorus Gregoras was the most remarkable. He was born in about 1295 at Heraclea in Pontus. His parents died when he

[1] For the career of the Emperor John VI Cantacuzenus, see the summary in D. M. Nicol, *The Byzantine Family of Kantakouzenos (Cantacuzenus)* (Washington, 1968), pp. 35–103.

was a child, and he was brought up by his maternal uncle, the Metropolitan of Heraclea, who instilled in him a taste for learning and, when he was twenty, sent him to Constantinople with an introduction to the learned Patriarch, John Glykys. The Patriarch introduced him to Metochites, who took to him at once and soon showered on him the affection that his own delinquent sons had forfeited. Metochites in his turn introduced the young scholar to the Emperor Andronicus II. Soon he was the star in the company of *savants* that Andronicus gathered around him. He refused to take any position at Court, but agreed to go on a delicate embassy to Serbia in 1326. He never held any University Chair, preferring to run his own school: which probably gave him more freedom and more money. The fall of Andronicus II and of Metochites was a blow to him; but he won the respect of Andronicus III and the affection of the Grand Logothete John Cantacuzenus, while loyally continuing to visit his fallen friends. He supported Cantacuzenus when civil war broke out on the death of Andronicus III. In 1330 he won renown through a debate in which he demolished the Calabrian Greek Barlaam, in which his deductive reasoning was shown to be far superior to Barlaam's syllogistic method. It is possible that his victory was not quite as complete as he claimed; for Barlaam, who was a fine mathematician and one of the founders of modern algebra, continued to have his admirers. In 1334 he won still greater renown by his triumphant arguments against two Papal emissaries, the Dominicans Francesco of Camerino and Richard the Englishman. His troubles started in 1340, with the beginnings of the Palamite controversy. Though the attack against Palamite doctrines was initiated, ironically, by his detested opponent Barlaam, Gregoras too was strongly and sincerely opposed to them; and his opposition coloured the rest of his life. He quarrelled with Cantacuzenus because of it, and refused to keep silence, even though he thereby lost his school and suffered a period of imprisonment. Not knowing the Christian Fathers as well as he knew the Classics, he was convinced that Palamas was a dangerous innovating heretic. His many scientific works belong to his earlier years. As a mathematician he achieved very little, chiefly because, like Metochites, he disapproved of the new use of Arabic numerals. His chief interests were in acoustics, where he tried to supplement Ptolemy's standard work and conducted another controversy with Barlaam, and in astronomy, where his most remarkable achievement was his scheme to correct the Julian calendar and fix the date of Easter. In later life he devoted himself to polemical works on theology, attacking Palamism, and to his great History. This, like that of Cantacuzenus, is written in a clear and effective style, and is likewise really an apologia for his career. But he was far vainer than Cantacuzenus, and far less generous to his opponents. He maintained that he won every debate in which he took part; and anyone who disagreed with him was unscrupulous, ambitious and dishonest. As a result he is a vivid and entertaining but quite unreliable guide, far better as a historian on the period before his own lifetime, as he could view those years with a scholarly detachment. His vanity was redeemed by intellectual integrity and courage. He had many devoted friends whom he never deserted when they fell into disgrace, and he valued friendship highly. Yet when Cantacuzenus tried to be reconciled to him his intransigence wrecked the reconciliation.[1]

Gregoras's *bête noire*, Gregory Palamas, would not have wished to be rated as an intellectual, and ought not to be counted amongst the scholars. But he had in fact had a good education and possessed a powerful intellect; and he wrote his great theological works in a clear Classical style, reminiscent of that of the Cappadocian Fathers, whom he greatly admired. But, though he was himself suspicious of scholarship, he had friends among the scholars with whom he corresponded; and the controversy arising from his doctrines showed how little there was of a party line amongst the scholars. Palamas's opponents were led by Barlaam, who was at first more Orthodox than the Orthodox but later was converted to

[1] The best general modern work on Nicephorus Gregoras is Guilland's *Essai sur Nicéphore Grégoras* (see above, p. 21, n. 2). There is a good summary of his thought in Tatakis, *Philosophie Byzantine*, pp. 256–61.

the Roman Church: Gregoras, who was Barlaam's bitter enemy and who was strongly anti-Roman: the Patriarch John Calecas, who was despised by all the intellectuals: Akyndinus, a Bulgarian by birth, who had been Palamas's favourite pupil: Demetrius Cydones, who was a devoted friend to John Cantacuzenus and eventually a convert to Rome: and the Papal legate, Paul of Smyrna. The Palamite supporters included John Cantacuzenus himself, as well as his political enemies Apocaucus and the Empress-Mother Anna, though her liking for Palamas was personal rather than ideological, a number of highly educated scholars such as Nicholas Cabasilas and Theodore of Melitene, and nearly the whole monkish element in the Church. Palamas himself was censured by Gregoras for maintaining a friendly correspondence with the Grand Master of the Latin Knights of Rhodes.[1]

Palamas's austere attitude towards Classical studies was by no means shared by his followers. Isidore Boukheras, the Athonite monk who succeeded John Calecas as Patriarch, was a scholar highly respected by his humanist pupil Demetrius Cydones.[2] His namesake, Metropolitan of Thessalonica at the close of the century and an adherent of Palamism, declared that a

[1] For Palamas, see J. Meyendorff, *A Study of Gregory Palamas*, trans. from the French by G. Lawrence (London, 1964); also Meyendorff's French translation and valuable introduction and notes to Palamas's own great work, *In Defence of the Holy Hesychasts.*
[2] See Meyendorff, *A Study of Gregory Palamas*, pp. 34–5.

study of the ancients would inculcate moral virtue, as their characters were far nobler than those of the men of his time.[1] Theodore of Melitene, professor at the Patriarchal Academy and an ardent Palamite, wrote a comprehensive and up-to-date encyclopedia of astronomy, which showed full acquaintance with Persian and Arab research, as well as a didactic poem entitled *On Chastity*, in which the lady Prudence (Sophrosyne) leads the poet through her realm, and which is almost as encyclopedic.[2]

The greatest of these Palamites was Nicholas Cabasilas, who was born in Thessalonica in about 1320. His father's surname was Chamaetus, but he took the surname of his maternal uncle, Nilus Cabasilas, later Metropolitan of the city, who was his teacher. He grew up in the tradition of Joseph the Philosopher, combining a taste for mystical contemplation with a love for secular learning. Nicholas Cabasilas's letters show his affection for Classical literature and science, though he wrote little himself on such subjects, apart from a

[1] Isidore's views are given in an unpublished sermon quoted in Tafrali, *Thessalonique au quatorzième siècle*, p. 157, n. 4, from MS. Gr. Paris 1192.

[2] See Krumbacher, *Byzantinischen Litteratur*, pp. 782–4. Krumbacher considers it impossible to say which member of the Meleniotes family wrote the poem, as no first name is given. But the whole nature of the work, which includes a rather pedantic account of the properties of precious stones and minerals, accords with Theodore's known interest in astronomy and mathematics, as well as poetry. For his scientific work, see Sarton, *History of Science*, III, part 2, 1512–14.

commentary on some of Ptolemy's works. As we have seen, he was a pioneer in the new use of the term 'Hellene'. After some hesitation he became convinced of the rightness of Palamite theology; but his views on mysticism were not those of Palamas. He might be called a mystical humanist. He believed that mystical experience could best be reached by concentration on the Sacrament, and that there was no reason why a mystic should not be a man of the world, and that secular learning would help rather than hinder him. Of all the Byzantine writers his style is the most attractive, combining Classical simplicity with a very individual grace, and even a sense of humour, as his unkind but witty attack on Gregoras and his pretensions reveals.[1]

The Thessalonian tradition that combined humanism and mysticism continued after Cabasilas's death. The sermons of the Metropolitan Isidore, written towards the end of the fourteenth century, are as yet unpublished, and, though he seems to have written in support of Palamite doctrines, that work has not survived. But he combined his mystical sympathies with Classical erudition and practical good sense. Symeon, who succeeded to the Metropolitan throne early in the fifteenth century, was perhaps less interested in Classical learning, but a much more distinguished theolo-

---

[1] For Cabasilas's life and teaching, see M. Lot-Borodin, *Un Maître de la spiritualité byzantine au XIVe siècle*; *Nicolas Cabasilas* (Paris, 1958). See also Tatakis, *Philosophie Byzantine*, pp. 277–81.

gian. His polemical works, against the Latins and against the anti-Palamites, show a moderation rare in that age. He was deservedly loved in Thessalonica, not only by the Greeks but also by the Italians and the Jews. His main work was an explanation of the symbolism contained in the Holy Liturgy and in the buildings in which the Liturgy took place. His theology of the Liturgy is not always in agreement with that of Cabasilas; his approach is less mystical, and it is the symbol which he regards as important. But his erudition about the Liturgy is vast, and his information is of great historical interest.[1]

Amongst the boys who sat with Nicholas Cabasilas at the feet of his uncle Nilus was Demetrius Cydones, who belonged to a rich family of Cretan origin, a family ruined by the Zealot rising. Isidore Boukheras had been for a time the family tutor. But Cydones turned against the Thessalonian contemplative tradition. He went to Constantinople, where he made a deep impression on John Cantacuzenus, henceforward one of his dearest friends. At Constantinople he learnt Latin from a Spanish Dominican living at Pera. Henceforward, apart from a few funeral orations and eulogies, and theological tracts mainly directed against the Palamites, his literary output consisted of translations from the Latin: of which the most important was his version of

---

[1] For Symeon, see M. Jugie, 'Symeon de Thessalonique', in *Dictionnaire de théologie catholique*, XIV, part 2, cols. 2976–84.

the *Summa Contra Gentiles* of Thomas Aquinas. This work, though it never circulated widely, aroused great interest in Constantinopolitan intellectual circles. Many Byzantine scholars, not all of them in favour of union with Rome, were fascinated by Western scholasticism. In his later years Cydones made several journeys to Italy, where he had many friends and admirers. He became a convert to the Roman Church while remaining a loyal Byzantine. In extreme old age he retired to a monastery in the Venetian-held island of Crete, from which his family had come. He was a lucid and able writer and a man of great personal charm. He never allowed his anti-Palamite views to mar his friendship with John Cantacuzenus and his family, unlike his brother Prochorus Cydones, who quarrelled furiously with the ex-Emperor. But Prochorus had the embittering position of being the leader of the anti-Palamites in the Palamite stronghold of Mount Athos. Demetrius was loyally devoted to the Emperor Manuel II, though their religious views were far from identical. He could speak with admiration of his old tutor, Isidore Boukheras, in spite of his dislike of Isidore's policy as Patriarch. If he wrote a tract against his old master, Nilus Cabasilas, it was because he thought that Nilus had been unfair to him.[1]

[1] See Beck, *Kirche und theologische Literatur*, pp. 733–7; K. M. Setton, 'The Byzantine background to the Italian Renaissance', in *Proceedings of the American Philosophical Society*, C, part I (Philadelphia. 1956), 52–7; Krumbacher, *Byzantinischen Litteratur*, pp. 489–92.

At the close of the fourteenth century intellectual life at Constantinople was dominated by two figures, Manuel II and the head of the Patriarchal Academy, Joseph Bryennius. Manuel's interest in culture was shown by his reform of the University and the Academy. He knew Latin and insisted on its study at the University. He had travelled widely in the West, in search of allies, and had many Western friends, though he failed to win the material help that he sought. But he disagreed with Latin theology, and he doubted whether the union of the churches would be practicable or wise. He was a fine enough theologian to be able to argue with the professors at the Sorbonne on the *filioque* clause and win their respect if not their agreement. His written works were mainly on theology, and included an elegant tract on the Christian faith designed for a Turkish audience. He also produced an essay on kingship, which shows the influence of Marcus Aurelius, and several *jeux d'esprit*, including a fanciful, if somewhat platitudinous, dialogue between Timur the Tartar and the captive Sultan Bayezit. He was admired by the Turks as well as by the Western potentates whom he visited. In all he was perhaps the most attractive and likeable of all the Byzantine Emperors.[1]

[1] See Beck, *Kirche und theologische Literatur*, pp. 747–9. The only biography of Manuel, Berger de Xivrey, *Mémoire sur la Vie et les Ouvrages de l'Empereur Manuel Paléologue* (Académie des Inscriptions, vol. XIX, Paris, 1853), is still useful. See also E. Legrand, *Les Lettres de l'Empereur Manuel Paléologue* (Paris, 1893).

His friend Joseph Bryennius, who died in 1431, six years after Manuel, shared his general views. He was a fine teacher, under whose aegis the Patriarchal Academy seems to have outshone the University, though he probably lectured at both institutions. He, like Manuel, knew Latin well and was interested in scholasticism. But he remained staunchly loyal to Orthodoxy; and his theological works were mainly tracts attacking Roman doctrines and supporting Palamite hesychasm. He wrote little else; but his will, in which he bequeathed his library to Saint Sophia and listed the books in it, reveals his interest in all the sciences, particularly in mathematics, optics and music. We know, too, that he was puzzled and distressed by the decline of medical studies in Constantinople.[1]

Bryennius came from Sparta, which was then little more than a suburb of Mistra, the small provincial capital of the Despots of the Morea. But while he journeyed from the Peloponnese to Constantinople, his slightly younger contemporary, George Gemistus, self-surnamed Plethon, who had been born in Constantinople, travelled in the opposite direction, to Mistra, on the advice of the Emperor Manuel, to carry on his teaching far away from the watchful eyes of the Great Church of the Imperial city. Plethon was born in about 1355. It was in about 1393 that he moved to

[1] Beck, *Kirche und theologische Literatur*, pp. 749–50. See also N. B. Tomadakes, Ὁ Ἰωσὴφ Βρυέννιος (Athens, 1947).

Mistra, where he enjoyed the protection of the enlightened despot, Manuel's second son, Theodore, and his charming Italian wife, Cleope Malatesta. Plethon was the one scholar of the time who saw no difference between the Inner and the Outer Learning, and was quite ready to jettison established Christian doctrine in favour of his own philosophical system. He particularly disliked apophatic theology. God gave us reason, he said, in order that we should understand everything. He had little use for Constantinople and none for the Roman tradition of Empire. 'We are Hellenes by race and culture', he wrote. His reason was dominated by his devotion to Plato. He loathed Aristotle and held him responsible for the wrong-headedness of Christian doctrine. His aim was to save the Greek world by reforming it along Platonic lines. He sent his proposals, worked out in considerable detail, in memoranda to the Emperor. They dealt with the structure of society, with finance and taxation, with the armed forces, with agricultural policy and with education, all planned with a superb disregard to actual political conditions and to probable human reactions. Had his schemes been practicable they would have created an unpleasantly Fascist State; but at least they showed the workings of a courageously independent and original intellect. His religious views were even more startling, considering the times. George of Trebizond, who disliked him, declared that he openly advocated a religion which he declared to be neither Christian nor Muslim but akin to the old paganism, and which, he hopefully foresaw, the whole world would soon adopt. His book *On the Laws*, in which he expressed what he really thought on religion, was never published. Only a few extracts have survived. The full text was discovered after his death by the Despot of the Morea, Demetrius, shortly after the Turkish capture of Constantinople. Demetrius sent it to George Scholarius, who was now the Patriarch Gennadius. The Patriarch, as he read pages in which God was usually called Zeus and the Trinity consisted of a supra-essential Creator, the Mind of the world and the Soul of the world, and maybe in which doctrines more shocking still were aired, decided, rather reluctantly but not surprisingly, that the manuscript must be burnt.

Plethon, though he had many friends even among the scholars whom his views appalled, had little influence on his fellow-countrymen. Had the Empire survived, he might have had disciples to carry on his message. But Constantinople fell only two years after his death. It was on the West that he left his mark. The Emperor John VIII nominated him as one of the delegates to the Council of Ferrara–Florence. It was an inappropriate choice. Plethon had no use for religious debates. Much as he disliked the Greek Church, he disliked the Latin Church even more, and somehow avoided signing the Act of Union. But he greatly enjoyed himself in Florence, where he gave lectures on Plato to enraptured audiences. It was in Italy, not in Greece, that his memory was to be honoured.[1]

The same was true of his most distinguished pupil. Bessarion was born at Trebizond in 1403. He was educated in Constantinople, under the rhetorician George Chrysococcus, who was probably a grandson of the famous astronomer of the same name, and became a monk at the age of twenty. He spent some years at a monastery near Mistra, where he attended Plethon's classes. On his return to Constantinople he soon became renowned as a brilliant teacher of philosophy. He was chosen to be one of the delegates to the Council of Ferrara–Florence, and was appointed Metropolitan of Nicaea in order that he might have a proper status there. Though he could not approve of Plethon's religious eccentricity, he had learned from Plethon to love Plato; and, like Plethon, he had no use either for scholasticism or for apophatic theology. The latter dislike prevailed. At Florence he let himself be genuinely convinced by the doctrinal arguments of the Latins; but his conversion was largely cultural. He believed that not only the Empire but Byzantine civilization

---

[1] For Plethon, see F. Masai, *Plethon et le Platonisme de Mistra* (Paris, 1956), *passim*, and for a good summary of his philosophy, Tatakis, *Philosophie Byzantine*, pp. 281–305. His insistence that 'we are Hellenes' is recorded in his epistle to Manuel II, in Migne, *Patrologia Graeco-Latina*, vol. CLX, cols. 821–4. What survives of his work *On the Laws* is published as *Traité des Lois*, ed. C. Alexandre, with a translation by A. Pellisier (Paris, 1858).

itself could only survive in alliance with the West. The Greeks should not stand aloof from the burgeoning life of Renaissance Italy. They should play their part in it. He was bitterly disappointed to find that very few of his compatriots shared his views. The lack of sympathy that he found in Constantinople after his return from the Council induced him to go back to Italy; and he spent the rest of his distinguished career in the West. But, even as a Cardinal of the Roman Church, he always felt himself to be a Greek, sighing for Byzantium. No one was more generous and solicitous towards refugees from Constantinople after the Turkish conquest; and no one took more trouble to rescue Greek manuscripts from destruction and oblivion. But his own writings were destined for a Latin rather than a Greek reading public.[1]

At the Council Bessarion's chief opponent among the Greeks had been Mark Eugenicus, a monk who similarly had been raised to a Metropolitan see, that of Ephesus, on his appointment as a delegate. Mark was born in about 1292 and was educated under Bryennius at the Patriarchal Academy. He belonged to the apophatic tradition, which put him at a disadvantage when

---

[1] For the whole range of Bessarion's career, see L. Mohler, *Kardinal Bessarion als Theologe, Humanist und Staatsmann* (3 vols., Paderborn, 1923–42). For his philosophy, see the summary in Tatakis, *Philosophie Byzantine*, pp. 294–301. For an estimate of his effect on the Renaissance, Setton, 'Byzantine background to the Italian Renaissance' pp. 72–4.

arguing with the subtle Latin spokesmen. Within his limits he was himself learned; and even his opponents recognized his sincerity and his integrity. Alone of the Greek delegates at Florence he could not be persuaded to sign the Act of Union. His own writings were mostly in praise of Hesychasm, though late in life he interested himself in the problem of predestination and grace, attempting to introduce an element of relativity: as a result of which he found himself in friendly disagreement with his disciple, George Scholarius.[1]

When Mark Eugenicus died in 1444 his place as leader of the anti-unionists was taken by George Scholarius. Scholarius had been born in 1405. He studied for a while under Eugenicus, but was trained as a lawyer and became a Judge-General, in charge of the University. He learnt Latin very thoroughly and became an ardent admirer of Thomas Aquinas. This admiration and his general interest in Latin scholarship affected all his thinking and his methodology. It also led him into theological difficulties. He was a Palamite, but in order to reconcile Palamism with his scholastic tastes he blurred the Palamite distinction between essence and operation, considering the latter to be only formally finite but really infinite because it had the same being as essence which was infinite. Palamas would not have approved of that interpretation. Other-

---

[1] Beck, *Kirche und theologische Literatur*, pp. 755–60; Tatakis, *Philosophie Byzantine*, pp. 295–7.

wise his theology was traditional. In his dispute with Eugenicus over predestination he restated the doctrine proposed long ago by John of Damascus and generally accepted by the Orthodox Church, though it still has no fixed dogma on the problem. He wrote a number of philosophical works, but as a philosopher he was unlucky in his time. His commentaries on Aristotle are remarkable, for he not only knew the original text thoroughly and the Greek commentaries but also the Latin commentaries by Gilbert de la Porrée, Albertus Magnus and Aquinas, and he had studied the works of Averrhoes and Avicenna. Had he and Bessarion exchanged their views on Church union and had he settled in Italy, he would certainly have influenced Italian scholarship and might have inaugurated a Neo-Aristotelian school at once more traditional and more profound than that which was later to arise at Padua.

He went as a lay delegate to the Council of Florence and there supported the union. On his return to Constantinople he began to have doubts. Eugenicus persuaded him that he had been theologically in error; but he was probably influenced still more by political considerations, doubting, with good reason, whether the West would or could send the help necessary to preserve Constantinople. He also seems to have believed, half ashamedly, that the end of the world was at hand. By Byzantine calculations the world would reach its 7,000th birthday in 1492—a year which was indeed a turning-point—and certainly Anti-Christ was at the gates. In such circumstances was the preservation of the earthly Empire of any importance? It mattered more that the Faith should be kept pure. The Byzantine world did indeed end soon afterwards, in 1453; and it was Scholarius's finest achievement that as the Patriarch Gennadius he worked out with the conquering Sultan a constitution which, for all its oppressive clauses, did preserve the entity of the Greek people and of their Church.[1]

There were other distinguished members of that last remarkable generation of Byzantine scholars. Many of them retired to Italy and there made their mark. But even now, when there was a definite unionist party amongst them and a party that opposed union, their incorrigible individualism still flourished. Plethon the Platonist opposed union. His Platonist pupil Bessarion warmly supported it. Scholarius, the Aristotelian with scholastic sympathies, succeeded the apophatically minded Eugenicus as leader of the anti-unionists. The Aristotelian George of Trebizond favoured union but disliked Bessarion. The Platonist George Amiroutzes of Trebizond at first supported union, then changed his mind and sought to find a synthesis between Christianity and Islam. Even in the last agony of Byzantium each of its scholars went his own individual way.

[1] Beck, *Kirche und theologische Literatur*, pp. 760–3; Tatakis, *Philosophie Byzantine*, pp. 295–9. For his later career see Runciman, *Great Church in Captivity*, pp. 168–70, 182–6, 193–4.

4

THE ACHIEVEMENTS OF
THE RENAISSANCE

IF SCHOLARS ARE men who study seriously and reflect upon their studies and seek to make deductions
from them, then these Byzantine intellectuals were
scholars. But what did their scholarship achieve? Did
they add anything of value to the sum of human knowledge and understanding?

For the results of learning to be effective, they have
to be transmitted, not only to the scholars' immediate
circle but in such a way that they can have meaning for
posterity. Herein the late Byzantine scholars were
unlucky. They were living in the declining years of a
civilization. In a short time Byzantium would perish
and the Greeks become second-class citizens. The
language in which they wrote was understood by few of
their contemporaries outside the shrinking Greek
world. By the time that Greek philology was studied in
the Western countries with which the future lay,
Byzantium had disappeared and its scholars were dispersed or dead. And, with the wealth of ancient Greek
literature and thought made available to them, Western
scholars were uninterested in what the later Greeks

might have had to say, unless it was closely relevant to the Classical past. Moreover, what the later Greeks had to say in general was restricted by their distinction between the Inner and the Outer Learning. The Inner Learning dealt with eternity, with truths that had existed before the beginning of time; and man could only know what God in His goodness had chosen to reveal. The rest was unknown and unknowable. The student of the Inner Learning might be able to expound and explain these revealed truths, but he could not add to them unless the Holy Spirit vouchsafed further revelations. The mystic might be permitted to penetrate a little further into the unknown but his experience was not an intellectual exercise. Even so devoted an advocate of philosophy as Nicephorus Gregoras could write that: 'All human opinion is but a symbol of ignorance.'[1] The sophists who arrogantly explained the universe in terms intelligible to the intellect had no place in Byzantium. Philosophy could not open the door into the Inner Learning.

Nevertheless, philosophy had its rôle. It could teach, not what to think but how to think. It could not explain heaven, but it could help to explain the earth. It was proper for the philosopher to turn his trained mind on to what now are called the sciences, as well as mathematics. Whether or not it was due to their philoso-

---

[1] Nicephorus Gregoras, *Florentios*, ed. A. Jahn, in *Jahns Jahrbuch*, Supplementband, 10 (Halle, 1844), pp. 531–2

phically trained minds the scientists of the last Byzantine period were amongst the foremost of their age. To us who live amidst vast scientific advance their achievements must seem absurdly petty. But in the context of the middle ages they were not to be despised. The Byzantine scholars had the advantage of being Greeks, brought up to be familiar with those Greeks of the past who had laid the foundations of scientific studies. Moreover, for all its intellectual pride and voiced contempt of the barbarians, Greek civilization had always been eclectic. Like their Classical ancestors the Byzantines were ready to learn and adapt knowledge from neighbouring peoples. Their religion came from Palestine, their law from Rome, their ceremonies mostly from Persia, and some of their ceremonial trappings even from China. They had constantly exchanged ideas and art-forms with the Muslim East. In this last period they even discovered, thanks above all to Planudes and to Demetrius Cydones, that there was something to be learnt from the long-despised West. There were, it is true, chauvinists like Theodore Metochites who maintained that Hellenic culture had no longer any need to borrow from elsewhere;[1] but in fact the borrowing was frequent and useful, and Metochites's own work would have been better had he been less xenophobe.

[1] 'Be a Hellene. Leave aside the theories of the Indians or the Scythians or the Persians.' Quoted from Metochites's commentary on Aristotle's *Physica*, in K. Sathas, Μεσαιωνικὴ Βιβλιοθήκη, I (Venice, 1872), preface, pp. πη′–πθ′.

7-2

Eclecticism by itself is ineffectual, but when allied to a strong native tradition it helps to keep that tradition alive.

In any case the old tradition remained dominant. The mathematicians of the time continued to paraphrase the works of Euclid and Nicomachus and Diophantus, works which had been somewhat neglected since the eleventh century; and their work was only carried forward by the use of Arabic numerals. As we have seen, Pachymer knew of them and Metochites chose to ignore them; and it was Planudes who by writing his *Calculation by the Indian Method* explained the system for Greek users. It was not readily adopted. Nicholas Rhabdas, the best mathematician of the next generation, seems to have used Arabic numerals in his calculations but when writing employed the old figures. It was only after the beginning of the fifteenth century that the new numerals, with a symbol for zero and decimal points, came into general use in Byzantine textbooks. Incidentally, though an anonymous Greek manuscript, dated 1252, of which Planudes certainly had a copy, makes use of the Gobar numerals, adopted by Western mathematicians, Planudes and his disciples took over the Eastern numerals, in use amongst the Persians and the Arabs of the Orient. Algebra, though it was known in Constantinople in the fourteenth century, chiefly through the teaching of the Calabrian Barlaam, never became a fashionable study there. The Byzantines much preferred logistics, geometry and geodesy, subjects which they put to good practical use, above all in architecture. They delighted in mathematical puzzles and riddles, which constituted a favourite after-dinner pastime; but though as a result they worked out many ingenious numerical problems, their contributions to mathematical theory were insignificant.[1]

In astronomy, too, the old tradition was revitalized by borrowings from the East. Serious astronomical study seems to have been revived in Constantinople by Michael Bryennius; and it was his pupil, Theodore Metochites, who made it popular. But Metochites's own work is little more than an introductory commentary on Ptolemy's *Syntaxis*. The advances in astronomy came from the scholars of Trebizond, where Persian and Arabic works, themselves based on Ptolemy but with the addition of later observations, were compared and synthesized with the writings of the ancients. These oriental treatises were collected by Choniades and were translated under his supervision by the monk Manuel of Trebizond and by his pupil George Chrysococces. The fullest synthesis was then made in Constantinople by Theodore of Melitene, professor at the Patriarchal Academy. His *Three Books on Astronomy* contains nothing remarkably original; but it is a compendium, which is still of value, of all the astronomical knowledge

---

[1] See K. Vogel, 'Byzantine Science', chapter xxviii in *Cambridge Medieval History*, iv, part 2 (new edition, Cambridge, 1967), 274–9; Sarton, *History of Science*, ii, part 2, 972–4, iii, part 1, 679–82.

available at the time.[1] But meanwhile Nicephorus Gregoras had made his one really original contribution to learning in his suggestions for the reform of the Julian calendar, worked out so as to give a universally acceptable date for Easter. He was not the first to make the attempt. There was already in Byzantium a work, attributed for no good reason to Saint John of Damascus, which dealt with the subject; and it had been more recently discussed in the West by John of Santobosco and a little later by Grosseteste and Roger Bacon. But Gregoras's work was impressively lucid and well-thought-out. The old Emperor Andronicus II was convinced of its merits. But it would have needed courage to take action on it; and before Andronicus could think of doing so he was dethroned, and the matter was dropped. Gregoras's rival, Barlaam, also wrote a small book on the subject, but with an equal lack of success. It is ironical to reflect, in view of the bitter hostility shown by the Orthodox to the reform of the calendar by Pope Gregory XIII, that, had Andronicus II been younger, more enterprising and more secure on the throne, the Orthodox authorities might have introduced an almost identical reform two centuries earlier.[2]

In the physical sciences the Byzantines, in common

---

[1] See Pingree, 'Gregory Choniades and Palaeologan Astronomy', *Dumbarton Oaks Papers*, no. 18, for a good discussion of Palaeologan astronomy, and Vogel, 'Byzantine Science' in *Cambridge Medieval History*, vol. IV.

[2] See Guilland, *Essai sur Nicéphore Grégoras*, pp. 279–85.

with everyone else in the middle ages, suffered from making their deductions from casual observation rather than from experiments. Where the subject was susceptible to mathematical treatment, as with mechanics or optics or acoustics, they were not hindered by this limitation; but in fact their work on these subjects was seldom more than a re-statement of what had been already stated. Michael Bryennius's great book on musical theory is a valuable compendium of the knowledge of the time; and both Pachymer and Metochites wrote observantly on optics. But their methods prevented any advance in chemistry, except on a purely technological and practical level, as in making dyes or glass; nor did they achieve anything in physics or in meteorology.[1]

In medicine, where careful observation is of value, the Byzantines, while they remained firmly entrenched in the tradition of Galen, added considerably to knowledge. As in astronomy, the scholars of Trebizond translated works from the Persian and the Arabic, which were of practical use. But there was original work also. The Nicaean Court physician, Nicholas Myrepsus, wrote a work on *materia medica*, which was for some centuries consulted in the West as well as in the East. Michael VIII's physician, Demetrius Pepagomenus, wrote a book on gout, based mainly on his own observations. He was also the author of a book on falconry, based equally on his own experience and

[1] Vogel, 'Byzantine Science', pp. 282–8.

notes. The most remarkable doctor of the period was the Court physician to Andronicus III, John Actuarius. He was an authority on diseases of the urine, about which he had much that was new to say. He seems to have been the first doctor to discover the whipcord, *trichocephalus dispar*, in the human intestine; and he was a pioneer in the study of psychosomatic complaints. After his time Byzantine medicine declined. At the end of the century Joseph Bryennius sadly recorded that medical practice was entirely in the hands of Jews.[1]

In geography the Byzantines added little to what Ptolemy had taught. Few of them were travellers; and their interest in foreign countries had usually been political and diplomatic rather than geographical. There were cartographers amongst them, particularly in these last centuries, when Muslim maps were studied, again, it seems, owing to the enterprise of the scholars of Trebizond. They were interested in the practical side, studying navigation and continually re-charting their home-waters. The compass seems to have been introduced into Byzantine ships in the fourteenth century. But it probably came to Byzantium from Italy.[2]

The occult sciences flourished in every period of

[1] *Ibid.* pp. 291–4; Sarton, *History of Science*, II, part 2, 1094–6, III, part 1, 859–92. Myrepsus's *Dynameron*, translated into Latin by Nicholas of Reggio, was the standard pharmocopia in use at Paris till the seventeenth century.

[2] See Guilland, *Essai sur Nicéphore Grégoras*, p. 276: Vogel, 'Byzantine Science', pp. 294–5.

Byzantine history. There were always fortune-tellers in Constantinople, adept at making their own fortunes even if they made no one else's: such as the imposter whom the Empress Anna liked to consult and whom Gregoras exposed. But, unlike Psellus and his friends, the scholars of this last period had no truck with occultism. They were superstitious. Even so learned a scholar as George Scholarius was affected by prophecies of the coming end of the world.[1] Nearly all of them were fascinated by the Pythagorean attitude to numbers. The fourteenth-century scholar Pediasimus even believed that certain numbers had a physiological effect.[2] But Metochites was anxious that no one should confuse astronomy with astrology, though his pupil Gregoras believed that the moon and stars did exercise an influence on human life.[3] The physicians of the time, such as Papagomenus and John Actuarius, were anxious to show that amulets and magical rites had no place in medicine. This refusal of the scholars to have any truck with occultism was one of the reasons for their good relations with the Church.[4]

[1] George Scholarius Gennadius, *Oeuvres Complètes*, ed. L. Petit and others (Paris, 1928–36), III, 161, 287, IV, 280–1.
[2] See Tatakis, *Philosophie Byzantine*, pp. 242–3.
[3] Guilland, *Essai Sur Nicéphore Grégoras*, pp. 277–8. In his pamphlet against Gregoras written in 1355 (ed. A. Garzya, 'Un opuscule inédit de Nicolas Cabasilas', in *Byzantion*, XXIV, Brussels, 1954, 521–32), Cabasilas laughs at Gregoras for giving himself the airs of a prophet, quoting Chaldean oracles and magical incantations.
[4] The flourishing superstitions in Byzantium at the beginning of the fifteenth century are denounced in a tract of Joseph Bryennius, cited

The scholars themselves would have doubtless regarded their philosophical works as their chief contributions to learning. Later generations cannot share that view. Byzantine philosophy was hampered not only by the need to keep clear of theology but also by their devotion to the Classical philosophy. 'The great men of the past', Metochites writes in the preface to his *Miscellanea*, 'have said everything so perfectly that they have left nothing for us to say.' All that one can do, he opines, is to make comments on them out of one's own experience. In some ways he does himself an injustice. In the course of his critical and appreciative remarks on more than seventy authors, of which the Christian Platonist, Synesius of Cyrene, seems really to have been his favourite, he managed to make his own individual thinking clear, though it turns out to be a rather unadventurous Platonism, muted by his piety. His comments show shrewdness and understanding and are to the point, in so far as they are not made unintelligible by the bewildering elaboration of his style.[1]

Though every Byzantine philosopher with the exception of Plethon would have subscribed to Metochites's view, a few were a little more enterprising. In

in L. Oeconomos, 'L'Etat intellectuel et moral des Byzantins vers le milieu du XIVe. siècle', in *Mélanges Charles Diehl* (Paris, 1930), I, 225–34. Oeconomos's title is misleading, as the tract must have been written after 1400.

[1] Theodore Metochites, *Miscellanea Philosophica et Historica*, ed. C. G. Muller and T. Kiessling (Leipzig, 1821), pp. 14–16 (see above, p. 65, n. 1).

the thirteenth century Blemmydes tried to reconcile medieval nominalism and realism by explaining that species exist eternally in the mind of God, and it is from them, having pre-determined them, that He has created all entities. His theory was studied and developed later by Bessarion and through him transmitted to the West.[1] Blemmydes's pupil, the Emperor Theodore II, deserves to be called an original thinker at least in his attitude towards nature, but the complication of his language obscures his thought.[2] Of the later philosophers, Joseph the Philosopher is interesting for his attempt to show the interconnection of all branches of science and learning and their relevance to Inner Learning:[3] and Chumnus for his refutation of Plato and of Plotinus, whose works he is one of the few Byzantines to have read, although he was defeated by Metochites's defence of Plato.[4] For all his learning, Gregoras was more of a rhetorician than a philosopher, as Cabasilas unkindly pointed out. He is of interest for his lofty views on the importance of history, which, like Metochites before him, he considered to be an essential study for the guidance of mankind. It not only explained the past but gave clear indications for the future. It showed the workings of nemesis and the

---

[1] Nicephorus Blemmydes, *Opera*, in Migne, *Patrologia Graeco-Latina*, vol. CXLII, col. 761.
[2] Theodore Lascaris, *Synopsis Sexti Sermonis*, in Migne, *Patrologia Graeco-Latina*, vol. CXL, cols. 1266 ff. (see above, p. 57, n. 1).
[3] See above, p. 66 and n. 1.   [4] See above, p. 63 and n. 1.

punishments meted out to nations for their crimes and apostasies. He thus combined something of both the Classical Greek and the Old Testament point of view; but he admitted also that the workings of providence were inscrutable: which weakened his argument.[1]

It was in the sphere of the Inner Learning that fourteenth-century Byzantium produced its finest philosophical work. Gregory Palamas did not regard his writings as being concerned with philosophy or as being original. He believed that he was merely expounding divine truths that were part of holy tradition. But his books on Hesychasm were the product of a formidable intellect expressed with a lucidity rare amongst Byzantines and are of prime importance in the history of religious thought. Less formidable but more charming are the works of his follower, Nicholas Cabasilas, the humanist mystic, who wished that the human intellect as well as the human soul should find expression, carrying on the tradition of Joseph the Philosopher into the Inner Learning. His *Life in Jesus*, which George Scholarius called a 'jewel of the Church,' is one of the finest works in Christian devotional literature. It is sad that it is so little known outside the world of Orthodox scholarship.[2]

The translation of Aquinas's works into Greek came too late in Byzantine history to affect the scholars of

---

[1] See Guilland, *Essai sur Nicéphore Grégoras*, pp. 230–6, for a summary of Gregoras's views on history. [2] See above, pp. 70-1.

Byzantium, with the one great exception of George Scholarius. The translator, Demetrius Cydones, was himself more of an elegant essayist than a philosopher. But with Scholarius we see the direction that Byzantine scholarship might have taken had Byzantium endured. But though he had his heirs in the West in the Neo-Aristotelian school of Padua, it was, rather, his philosophical opponent Plethon and his philosophical and ecclesiastical opponent Bessarion who were to bring the influence of Byzantium to bear on the West.[1]

As literary figures these scholars of latter-day Byzantium left no legacy. They wrote for the most part in a sophisticated language for a sophisticated public which was soon to be wiped out. The future in Greek letters lay with the popular writers using a popular tongue. But if we regard scholarship as providing a great compendium of human knowledge which is available for those who choose to consult it, even if many of the chapters remain unread, then these scholars made a real contribution to scholarship. But if it is the duty of scholarship to play a part in the general stream of learning, then their contribution was limited; and, ironically, it lay in the area which to most of us today was its least interesting side. It was for those endless commentaries of the ancient philosophers that the scholars of Byzantium made their mark on the scholars of Renaissance Italy.

[1] See above. pp. 80-1.

The Fourth Crusade and the Francocratia in Greece, for all the political harm that they did to Byzantium and to Europe, had one compensating result. They brought Westerners into Greek lands and enabled them to see a living Greek culture from close at hand. The conquering Franks were for the most part simple warriors with no understanding of the civilization of the people whom they had conquered. But the century of the conquest was the century in which the scholars of the West first became properly aware of the wealth of ancient Greek learning. They received it in translations from the Arabic. But it gradually dawned on them, as an outcome of their closer connection with the Greek world, that in that world these valued writings were to be found in their original tongue and were still read and studied. Even the schism between the Churches helped to create this awareness; for Rome now sent missionaries who were to heal the breach and chose for that purpose men of good education. In particular Rome liked to make use of priests of Greek birth who had been converted to the Latin Church and who were therefore well fitted to bring the two cultures together. Men like Nicholas of Cotrone or John Parastron in the thirteenth century and Paul of Smyrna and Simon Atumano in the fourteenth, and even the volatile Barlaam of Calabria, though they may not have secured the conversion of many of their countrymen, could at least inform the West of Greek scholarship. Cultured Italians in the fourteenth century began to want to learn Greek. Petrarch himself had a few lessons from Barlaam, though he proved to be a poor pupil.[1] In 1204 the Franks had happily made bonfires of Greek manuscripts snatched from the libraries of Constantinople. Two centuries later their descendants were sending agents to buy such manuscripts at whatever price might be asked for them.

It was some time before Greek scholars, apart from the converts, visited the West. George Acropolites attended the Council of Lyons. Planudes went on an embassy to Venice.[2] But neither of them made lasting intellectual contacts. Barlaam on his return to Italy was more effective; but, for all his talents, he was suspect on both sides.[3] The Emperor John V's visits to Italy in search of political and financial aid were unproductive of intellectual results, except that he brought Demetrius Cydones with him. The arrival of Demetrius Cydones in Italy opened a new era. He was a scholar respected for his translations from the Latin, who liked to move amongst scholars; and he was a man of great personal charm. He made an excellent ambassador for Byzantine learning.[4] Soon, largely through his in-

[1] See Setton, 'Byzantine background to the Italian Renaissance', *Proceedings of the American Philosophical Society*, C, part 1, esp. pp. 40–52.
[2] See above, pp. 58–60.
[3] Setton, 'Byzantine background to the Italian Renaissance', pp. 44–5.
[4] See above, p. 75 and n. 1.

fluence, his friend and pupil Manuel Chrysoloras was invited to lecture on the Greek philosophers at Florence. Chrysoloras was not a very profound scholar, but he seems to have been a lecturer who could inspire his audiences. He instilled in the Florentines a taste for the divine Plato; and they longed to learn more.[1] The Emperor Manuel, himself a fine scholar, helped further to raise Byzantine intellectual prestige even beyond the frontiers of Italy. His debating powers greatly impressed the doctors at the Sorbonne; and the unintellectual English recognized him as a man of high culture.[2] Meanwhile Italian scholars began to visit Constantinople, not just to conduct religious discussions but to listen to Greek scholars. Men like the able if unadmirable Francesco Filelfo spent many months at its schools.[3] The future Pope Pius II tells us that in his youth every aspiring student wanted to make the journey.[4] The Council of Florence further whetted the Italian appetite, when Plethon, whom all the Greek visitors declared to be the greatest of living Platonists, came to the city and, being bored by the interminable religious debates at the Council, spent his time giving lectures on Plato: to such effect that Cosimo de' Medici founded a

[1] Setton, 'Byzantine background to the Italian Renaissance' pp. 57–8.
[2] See above, p. 76.
[3] For Filelfo, see Setton, 'Byzantine background to the Italian Renaissance', pp. 72–3, and D. Geanakoplos, *Greek Scholars in Venice* (Cambridge, Mass., 1962), pp. 32–3.
[4] Pius II, Pope, *Opera Omnia* (Basle, 1551), p. 681.

Platonic Academy in his honour.[1] Less sensational but
more effective than Plethon was his most distinguished
disciple Bessarion, who retired to Italy towards the end
of 1440, and there published his most important book,
Against the Calumniators of Plato, which had a great
influence on the whole thought of the Renaissance. The
imminence of the fall of Constantinople and then the
fall itself brought other Greek scholars to Italy, where
they continued the debate, so well enjoyed in Byzantium, on the respective merits of Plato and Aristotle.
The leading Aristotelians were Theodore of Gaza,
Andronicus Callistus and George of Trebizond, and
the leading Platonists John Argyropoulos, Michael
Apostolis and Bessarion himself. Thanks chiefly to
Bessarion Platonism triumphed.[2] But Aristotelianism
had its victory later, when in 1497 the Epirot Nicholas
Laonicus Thomaeus, who seems to have studied the
works of Scholarius, began to lecture at Padua on
Aristotle, using nothing but the Greek text and Greek
commentaries. These lectures, which the future
Cardinal Bembo regarded as opening a new era in
Western philosophy, led in due course to the Neo-
Aristotelianism of Pomponazzi and Cremonini: which
in its turn opened the door to the uninhibited study of
the sciences in the century to come. Perhaps more im-

[1] For Plethon's visit to Florence and his influence on the Italian
humanists, see Masai, *Pléthon et le Platonisme de Mistra*, pp. 315 ff.
[2] See Tatakis, *Philosophie Byzantine*, pp. 290, 293–5, 299–301.

portant still, these refugee Greek scholars, with Bessarion at their head, took trouble to collect and to copy the Greek manuscripts that Byzantium had preserved.[1]

It was from these scholars, these Platonicians and Aristotelians alike, that the men of the Renaissance learnt most of their philosophy. The immediate results were not very lively to our way of thinking. The philosophical works of the Italian Renaissance for the most part can challenge those of the Byzantines for uninspired verbosity. But they carried on the tradition, to inspire more original minds in the future. The Byzantines have been called 'the librarians of the middle ages'.[2] They conserved ancient books worthy of conservation, and some that were unworthy; and they read them and commented on them, and transmitted what they had conserved for the benefit of European civilization.

But there were other sides of Byzantine life which could not survive the fall of the city in which that life was centred. The practical techniques, the mechanics and the like in which the Byzantines excelled, could no longer be developed. The art, the noblest expression of Byzantine civilization, was halted and stunted because it no longer quite knew what it wished to express. Even

---

[1] See Geanakoplos, *Greek Scholars in Venice*, pp. 136–8 and P. Sherrard, *The Greek East and the Latin West* (London, 1959), pp. 125–7.

[2] N. H. Baynes, *Byzantine Studies and other Essays* (London, 1955), pp. 71–2.

the deep religious feelings of the Greeks became some-what atrophied without the concept of the holy Empire of God on earth to inspire them. The fall of Constantinople truly marked the end of a long story, the end of a great civilization; and little was able to endure there except for crumbling buildings, falling mosaics and fading frescoes, and memories of an idea of the world that could not be maintained. It was the treasures that Byzantium had eagerly and carefully preserved that were handed on, not the conception of Byzantium itself. Yet during those last centuries of political decadence and of thickening gloom, the intellectual torch had burned brightly. The scholarship of the last Byzantine Renaissance may not mean much to us today. But the scholarship was there, genuine and intense; and it deserves our respect.

FURTHER READING

GENERAL WORKS

Further information about the scholars mentioned in this book can be found in the sources cited below.

BECK, H.-G. *Kirche und theologische Literatur im Byzantinischen Reich*. Munich, 1959.

BRÉHIER, L. *Le Monde byzantin*. 3 vols., Paris, 1947–50.

Cambridge Medieval History. Vol. IV, 2 parts, new ed., Cambridge, 1966–7.

FUCHS, F. *Die Höheren Schulen von Konstantinopel im Mittelalter*. Leipzig, 1926.

KRUMBACHER, K. *Geschichte der Byzantinischen Litteratur*. 2nd ed., Munich, 1897.

SARTON, G. *Introduction to the History of Science*. Vols. I–III, Baltimore, 1927–48.

SETTON, K. 'The Byzantine background to the Italian Renaissance'. *Proceedings of the American Philosophical Society*, vol. C. Philadelphia, 1956.

TAFRALI, O. *Thessalonique au quatorième siècle*. Paris, 1913.

TANNERY, P. *Sciences exactes chez les Byzantins; Mémoires scientifiques*. Vol. IV, Paris, 1920.

TATAKIS, B. *La Philosophie Byzantine*, fascicule supplémentaire, no. II, in E. Bréhier, *Histoire de la Philosophie*. Paris, 1949.

WORKS ON INDIVIDUAL SCHOLARS

BECK, H.-G. *Theodoros Metochites. Die Krise des byzantinischen Weltbildnes im 14 Jahrundert*. Munich, 1952.

GUILLAND, R. *Essai sur Nicéphore Grégoras*. Paris, 1926.

Further reading

LOT-BORODIN, M. *Un Maître de la spiritualité byzantine au XIVe siècle; Nicolas Cabasilas*. Paris, 1958.

MASAI, F. *Pléthon et la Platonisme de Mistra*. Paris, 1956.

MEYENDORFF, J. *A study of Gregory Palamas*, trans. G. Lawrence. London, 1964.

ŠEVČENKO, I. *Études sur la Polémique entre Théodore Métochite et Nicéphore Choumnos*. Brussels, 1962.

VERPEAUX, J. *Nicéphore Choumnos, Homme d'état et Humaniste Byzantin*. Paris, 1959.

INDEX

Index

Index

Index

Index

Index